The
FRIENDSHIP
BOOK

of Francis Gay

D. C. THOMSON & CO., LTD.
London   Glasgow   Manchester   Dundee

A Thought
For Each Day
in 1994

Friendship is love with understanding.

A LESSON FOR LIFE

JANUARY

SATURDAY—JANUARY 1.

A S I walked down the road on this first day of January, it was very pleasant to be greeted by my neighbours wishing me a Happy New Year. The start of a new calendar with its clean, fresh pages is something we cannot ignore. It offers us a new beginning and it is good to wish one another peace and goodwill in the year ahead.

Whether or not we propose to make any New Year Resolutions, the end of one year and the beginning of another is inevitably a time for taking stock:

To look backward with gratitude;
To look onward with hope;
And to look upward with confidence.

Charles Lamb put it this way: "Every first of January that we arrive at is an imaginary milestone on the turnpike track of human life, at once a resting place for thought and meditation, and a starting point for fresh exertion in the performance of our journey."

A very Happy New Year to you!

SUNDAY—JANUARY 2.

F OR the Lord is good; his mercy is everlasting; and his truth endureth to all generations.

Psalms 100:5

MONDAY—JANUARY 3.

I LIKE the story of the three-year-old who went to church with his grandmother for the first time. The collection plate came round, and he was heard to whisper, "You don't have to pay for me, Gran. I'm not five yet!"

THE FRIENDSHIP BOOK

WHEN the New Year dawns, I take down our old calendar and put up a new one. If there is time, I sometimes sit and look through the comments beside days made over the past year. Where there are birthdays entered, I transfer them to the new calendar as a reminder. A whole new year lies ahead and I wonder what these 12 months will bring.

Sidney Carter, the songwriter, sums up my feelings well in his rousing hymn:

One more step along the world I go,
One more step along the world I know,
From the old things to the new,
Keep me travelling along with You.

NOT long ago, the Lady of the House and I were pruning a rose hedge in the garden when a neighbour and keen fellow gardener stopped to watch us and give advice.

"Don't forget to prune the dead wood," he said. "It will give the new shoots room to grow."

True enough, we found quite a lot of this and dealt with it as he advised.

There comes a time when we should prune the dead wood from our lives, too. Not everything we try to do can be a success and it's very easy to spend time dwelling on failures, and growing more and more miserable and lacking in confidence.

Prune out the mishaps, the bad habits, and learn by your mistakes — tackle something else, a completely new project. Once you have ceased to waste time, you will have more chance of succeeding with new ideas and schemes because you will be able to give them your undivided attention.

THE FRIENDSHIP BOOK

MY friend Bill is a shift worker and when he has a few minutes to spare in the daytime, he goes to have a chat with the old lady who lives across the road. They get on well together.

"One day, she confessed that she hadn't been sleeping at all soundly," Bill told me, "but she said that when she lay awake, she always thought about something nice."

"What sort of things do you think about?" he had asked.

"Oh, I think about you coming to see me and about all the nice conversations we have," replied his friend.

It had never dawned on Bill that his calls meant so much to her. "In fact," he laughed, "I sometimes wondered if she might be beginning to think I was a bit of a nuisance."

A good neighbour can never be that.

IT'S interesting to discover how phrases have changed their meaning over the years. An example is "talking through your hat" which nowadays is used in a derogatory sense and suggests that somebody doesn't really know what he or she is talking about.

However, in the 17th century men actually talked through their hats when they went to church. It was the custom to keep hats or hoods on in church during the service. On entering they would remove their headgear, and holding it in front of their mouths, would say a short prayer before replacing their hats on their heads and sitting down.

So, if you are ever tempted to accuse somebody of "talking through their hat", just spare a thought for its old meaning!

THE FRIENDSHIP BOOK

THIS is a nun's prayer from the 17th century, but it's just as valid today. See what you think:-

"Lord, thou knowest better than I know myself that I am growing older and that some day I will be old. Keep me from the fatal habit of thinking I must say something on every subject and on every occasion.

"Release me from craving to straighten out everybody's affairs; make me thoughtful, but not moody, helpful, but not bossy. With my vast store of wisdom, it seems a pity not to use it all; but thou knowest, Lord, that I want a few friends at the end.

"Keep my mind free from recital of endless details; give me wings to get to the point. Seal my lips on my aches and pains. They are increasing and love of rehearsing them is becoming sweeter as the years go by. I dare not ask for grace enough to enjoy listening to the tales of others' pains, but help me to endure them with patience.

"I dare not ask for improved memory, but for a growing humility and a lessening cocksureness when my memory seems to clash with the memories of others. Teach me the glorious lesson that occasionally I may be mistaken.

"Keep me reasonably sweet; I do not want to be a Saint — some of them are so hard to live with — but a sour old person is one of the crowning works of the devil. Give me the ability to see good things in unexpected places, and talents in unexpected people. And give me, O Lord, the grace to tell them so."

AND a certain scribe came, and said unto him, Master, I will follow thee whithersoever thou goest.

Matthew 8:19

THE FRIENDSHIP BOOK

DON'T ENVY

DON'T envy those who have much more
 For others may have less,
Comparing this should then restore
 Your faith and happiness.

Some are less fortunate than you
 In health or worldly things,
Counting your blessings, be strong and true
 See what contentment brings.

Dorothy M. Loughran.

MRS JONES called to have a cup of tea with the Lady of the House and tell her all her news. She was full of stories about the wedding of one of our young Sunday School teachers and had volunteered to help with the washing-up after the reception in the church hall.

"I noticed that the washing-up water was getting full of little bits of coloured paper," she said, "and I thought it's surprising where confetti manages to find its way. Then the bride's mother came through to thank me and said, 'We had to borrow a lot of crockery, of course, but it has all been marked with little coloured stickers underneath — blue for Mary's, green for Joan's and yellow for Enid's, so you won't have any problems sorting it out' . . ."

The unexpected in an apparently simple situation can often catch us unawares and we have to be ready to tackle the unforeseen in everyday life, no matter how trifling the hitch may be.

THE FRIENDSHIP BOOK

THAT great freedom fighter, Bishop Abel Muzarewa, once gave these words of advice to a group of African pastors.

People are unreasonable, illogical and self-centred.

Love them, anyway!

Honesty and frankness make you vulnerable.

Be honest and frank, anyway!

The biggest people with the biggest ideas can be shot down by the smallest people with the smallest ideas.

Think big, anyway!

What you spend years building may be destroyed overnight.

Build, anyway!

Although you give the world the best you have, you may still be kicked in the teeth.

Give your best, anyway!

I HAVE seen inside many different churches and have seen many beautiful stained glass windows and other ecclesiastical treasures over the years. It has often made me wonder about the nature of the real treasures of the church.

I recalled that when the early Christians were being harassed and persecuted by the Emperor Decius, he sent a messenger to demand that the congregation should hand over all its treasures to the State.

Their deacon, Laurentius, indicated the crowd of poor and sick people, some maimed and blind, who were being looked after by the Christian church in Rome, and nobly declared, "*These* are the treasures of the Church."

THE FRIENDSHIP BOOK

I DON'T know who wrote these words, but for me they seem to capture exactly the magic of a smile:

"A smile is something that costs nothing, but creates much. It enriches those who receive without impoverishing those who give. It happens in a flash, but the memory of it sometimes lasts for ever. None are so rich they can get along without it and none so poor, but both are richer for its benefits.

"It creates happiness in the home, fosters goodwill in business. It is rest to the weary, daylight to the discouraged, sunshine to the sad. It cannot be bought, begged, borrowed or stolen, it is something that is no earthly good to anybody until it is given away. Those who have none left to give are the ones who need one most."

In fact, it's a priceless treasure that costs nothing, so it's something we can afford to be generous with!

GARY PLAYER has been an important figure on the golf course for many years, and the winner of a number of international championships. His success hasn't been achieved without a great deal of hard work, and talking abut his achievements on a radio interview he said, "The more I practise, the luckier I get," and he went on to say that for 40 years he had never missed a day in the gymnasium, however disinclined or busy he might be.

Well, a workout in a gymnasium each day is not for everyone, but there's a lot to be said for deciding on our goal in life and then working steadily towards it. As Eleanor Roosevelt once said, "If we wait till we're ready, we never do anything."

THE FRIENDSHIP BOOK

IF ye abide in me, and my words abide in you, ye shall ask what ye will, and it shall be done unto you.

John 15:7

OUR neighbour's handsome Persian cat, which I'd been looking after for a day or two, accepted a saucer of milk from me, but afterwards declined my attempts to stroke him and stalked disdainfully down the garden path. As Gautier said, "A cat can be your friend, but never your slave."

In his amusing book of poetry, "Old Possum's Book of Practical Cats", T.S. Eliot wrote:

With Cats, some say, one rule is true:
Don't speak till you are spoken to.
Myself, I do not hold with that —
I say, you should ad-dress a Cat,
But always keep in mind that he
Resents familiarity.

There's a saying in Russia that if you want to be happy in a new home, a cat must move in with you, and I once read that cats are such peaceful creatures anyone who lives with them and watches them relax, rarely has high blood pressure.

Beryl Reid, the entertainer, is a great cat-lover whose home has been filled with cats for many years. In "The Cat's Whiskers" she wrote this dedication:

"Cats have struggled, sailed and forced their way through history. They have seen more ups and downs than any other animals, being adored and detested for 10,000 years, but they, rather like me, are survivors and refuse to be defeated or squashed by anything. That is why we, who love them, still continue to have the pleasure of their company."

Cat owners will know exactly what she means!

THE FRIENDSHIP BOOK

HOW pleasant it is to sit and daydream — as long as the dreams don't gain too much control over reality!

Dr Johnson said, "Life is not long and too much of it must not pass in idle deliberation on how it should be spent." On the same subject Christina Rossetti wrote, "Can anything be sadder than work left unfinished? Yes, work never begun." Ellen Thorneycroft Fowler's comment was, "It is better to build a cathedral than to make a boat; but I think it is better actually to make a boat than only to dream about building a cathedral."

However, on this topic of dreams versus reality, these anonymous lines will surely give us something to think about:

"The life of every one of us is a diary in which we mean to write one story and so often write another. Our most humble hour is when we compare the volume as it is with what we vowed to make it."

I'M sure most people are aware that "to bury the hatchet" means to be reconciled and let bygones be bygones.

The saying originates from factions of North American Indians who were commanded by their Great Spirit to cease hostilities, to come together for a pow-wow and bury all their instruments of war — hatchets, scalping knives, clubs and war drums — and sit down together smoking the peace pipe. During this time all hostile thoughts were to be put aside to concentrate on peaceful ones.

The actual form of the old custom has ceased now, although the peace pipe is still smoked, but it is always worth remembering the meaning of that old saying!

THE FRIENDSHIP BOOK

IT'S only a short word, but "hello" seems to be the key to making friends, especially on those sometimes difficult first meetings. This verse by Phyllis Ellison expresses my thoughts on the matter rather neatly.

A room full of strangers,
Should we tiptoe away?
With no-one we know,
We've no reason to stay.
Then clear as a bell,
Someone shouts out, "Hello!"
Pull up some chairs,
There's no need to go.

I MUST admit to enjoying the holiday programmes on television at this time of the year and dreaming of exotic, far-away places — Winter ski resorts, the mystery of the East and silvery palm-fringed beaches. What a variety of destinations there is!

Once I watched something more down-to-earth where a group of young people were on an Outward Bound course. During the week they helped each other to solve problems as they got to grips with sailing, rock climbing and abseiling, ending with a wet night's camping on a mountainside.

Afterwards, one of the girls reported that it had been hard work, but great fun. She added, "With the support of a good team behind you, you can overcome all your obstacles."

It's very much like life. As we go along the way — in good times and bad — whatever would we do without our family, friends and neighbours, and all who support us when we most need help?

THE FRIENDSHIP BOOK

THERE'S a lot to think about in these "Ten Commandments" for a happy marriage, whether we are just about to embark on ours — or if we think that by now we know all the answers!

1. Thou shalt not take thy partner for granted.
2. Thou shalt not expect perfection of each other.
3. Thou shalt be patient, loving, understanding, kind and true.
4. Thou shalt tend the garden of love daily.
5. Thou shalt take great care that thy partner's trust is never violated or diminished in any way.
6. Thou shalt not forget thy wedding vows, remembering especially those important words "for better or for worse".
7. Thou shalt not hide true feelings. Mutual love provides a bright, sunlit room where things of the heart can be discussed freely and without fear.
8. Thou shalt always respect each other as individuals. Degrading words and a sharp tongue cause grave distortions. Endearing terms ennoble, lift up, engender peace.
9. Thou shalt give thy marriage room to grow. Both partners should be willing to face the future together with confidence and trust. Today is a better day for them than yesterday, and tomorrow will find them closer still.
10. Thou shalt through all thy days reverence God, thy Creator, never forgetting that it is He who has made you.

THOU art worthy, O Lord, to receive glory and honour and power: for thou hast created all things, and for thy pleasure they are and were created.

Revelation 4:11

THE FRIENDSHIP BOOK

IN his book "Try Giving Yourself Away", David Dunn related an incident which happened as he travelled home on a rush-hour commuter train crowded with tired passengers. The brakes were applied very suddenly and if they hadn't been so tightly packed, people would have fallen over. As it was, Dunn had his feet stepped on and an elbow jabbed in his back.

In irritation he turned round and his fellow passenger said, "Terribly sorry, my friend," and then, in a voice loud enough to be heard down the carriage, he announced, "Unscheduled stop. All change for Good Nature!"

Straight away, said Dunn, the atmosphere changed as everyone had "a glimpse of the city as it *might be* — good natured, friendly, human."

WHEN she is stooped
And frail and old,
When bones are weak
And blood runs cold —
Hold her hand.
When he is trembling,
And sore distressed,
Fraught with fancies
And cannot rest —
Hold his hand.
When you are worried,
And oppressed with care
And sights of suffering
You can hardly bear.
Hold His hand.
                    Jean Harris.

THE FRIENDSHIP BOOK

WE recently called to see our friend Mary because we'd heard that she was laid up after a nasty fall.

Indeed, I found she had cut and bruised her leg when she had tripped over the doorstep and had needed a couple of visits to hospital to have it seen to. So there she was, resting her leg, swathed with dressings, on a footstool. I expressed my sympathy at her accident, but Mary greeted me with her usual cheerful smile.

"I'm not complaining," she said. "I have all the time in the world now to finish the book you gave me, I have no need to feel guilty about watching television in the morning — and although I can't walk, I can still enjoy eating all that delicious fruit I've been given."

As I've said before, it's not often that I come away after visiting Mary without hearing something to make me stop and think!

HERE are a few more items from my collection of 20-second sermons — those few words with a big message:

Today is the first day of the rest of your life. Don't waste it!

Remember, when life's path seems closed by obstacles — keep an open mind.

God promises a safe landing, but not a calm passage. (Bulgarian Proverb)

Forgiveness is the perfume cast back from a dying flower upon the foot that crushed it.

Love builds bridges which will last.

And (seen in a hospital waiting-room):

RELAX — God's in charge!

THE FRIENDSHIP BOOK

YOU WILL NEVER BE OLD

YOU will never be old
With a twinkle in your eye,
With the Springtime in your heart
As you watch the Winter fly.
You will never be old
While you have a smile to share,
While you wonder at mankind
And you find the time to care.
While there's magic in your world
And a special dream to hold,
While you still can laugh at life,
You never will be old.

Iris Hesselden.

THERE is something about unused sheets of paper that attracts me — notebooks, writing pads, typing paper, all blank and waiting to have things written on them, ideas, letters, lists and so on. At school I felt a thrill of anticipation when I opened a new exercise book — sometimes the pages were still uncut.

In the days before we all became conscious of environmental issues, I had a weakness for expensive deckle-edged writing paper. Nowadays, I buy recycled paper wherever possible, to save our woodlands.

Each day is like a fresh sheet of paper, isn't it? It is blank until we make the imprint of our lives upon it. If, on the previous day, things have not gone as planned and we have fallen short of our ideals, we can put it behind us, take up a new sheet and start again.

THE FRIENDSHIP BOOK

THEREFORE, my beloved brethren, be ye stedfast, unmoveable, always abounding in the work of the Lord, forasmuch as ye know that your labour is not in vain in the Lord.

Corinthians I 15:58.

IN 1952 a window was dedicated in a Chicago church. It is unique because although it was designed after the fashion of traditional stained glass, it is made entirely of pieces of jade — the world's only jade window.

It was the gift of James L. Kraft, founder of the well-known American food firm and also a committed Christian. The story began when, as a ploughboy, he turned up pieces of the precious stone, which so fascinated him that collecting it developed into a life-long hobby.

From earliest times this sacred stone of the Orient has symbolised truth, goodness and beauty, and Kraft's dream was to obtain sufficient American jade to place a window in the church where he worshipped, as a gift of the finest fruits of his hobby.

It took many years to find the different colours of jade required, but now the window is set in the east wall of the church where its many translucent segments reflect the morning sun. Twenty subtly-blended colours of jade make up the window, each piece cut and polished to about half the thickness of stained glass. The central cross which fills the window is made of rare, pure white jade, with a central rosette bearing the letters IHS, an abbreviation of the Greek letters for Jesus.

The poor ploughboy who became a millionaire could not have left a more beautiful memorial.

FEBRUARY

TUESDAY—FEBRUARY 1.

THAT cold month of January has been left behind and here we are in February once more. It's the shortest month of the year, days are noticeably growing longer and "Fair Maids of February" or "Candlemas Bells", better known as snowdrops, are showing themselves in sheltered corners of the garden.

On 1st February 1842 Coleridge wrote his poem "February" and I pass it on to you today as a reminder that Spring is on its way:

One month is past, another is begun,
Since merry bells rang out the dying year,
And buds of rarest green began to peer,
As if impatient for a warmer sun;
And though the distant hills are bleak and dun,
The virgin snowdrop, like a lambent fire,
Pierces the cold earth with its green-streaked spire
And in dark woods the wandering little one
May find a primrose.

WEDNESDAY—FEBRUARY 2.

CATHERINE GLYNNE was a lovely girl, but found it difficult to get over an unsuccessful love affair. One day, she was noticed by a young man of high principles who invited her to marry him.

She protested that she had only half a heart to offer him.

Her suitor replied, "Give it to me, and I will make it a whole one." So William Ewart Gladstone, one of our finest Prime Ministers, married the girl with whom he shared well over half a century of domestic happiness.

THE FRIENDSHIP BOOK

AT school one wet playtime five-year-old Ian fell over in the playground. He went back into school wet, weeping and covered in mud. His teacher came to the rescue.

"Ian, however did you manage to make such a mess of yourself?" she added.

"It was easy, Miss," came the reply.

Sometimes, maybe because of a wrong decision, or our own stupidity, life goes awry and we fall deeply into the mud. It's at times like this we should always remember that we have an even more concerned and Friendly Teacher than Ian's to pick us up, dust us down and set us on the road again.

TODAY I'd like to pass on this prayer I heard from our friend, Joanne. She says it has helped her a lot when she is feeling down — and I hope there will be a message in it for you too, today:

Dear God, when I am lonely, and when I feel despair,
Let not my ailing heart forget you hear my
every prayer.
Remind me that no matter what I do or fail to do,
There still is hope for me as long as I have hope
in You.
Let not my eyes be blinded by some folly I commit,
But help me to regret my wrong and to make up for it.
Inspire me now to put my fears upon a hidden shelf,
And in the future never to be sorry for myself.
Give me the restful sleep I need, before another dawn
And bless me in the morning with the courage
to go on.

                                        Anon.

FROST FANTASIA

SATURDAY—FEBRUARY 5.

ONE of the lesser-known saints is St Dorothy whose feast it is tomorrow.

According to legend, she was condemned to death because she refused to worship idols and was sent for execution in Caesarea. On the way, a young lawyer, Theophilus, mocked her and challenged her to send him fruits from the garden of Paradise to which she was going.

As Dorothy knelt in prayer, an angel appeared and gave Theophilus a basket containing three apples and three roses. When he tasted the fruit he was converted to Christianity.

St Dorothy can sometimes be seen in stained glass windows holding the basket of heavenly fruit and flowers, but I remember her appropriately as the Patron Saint of Gardens.

SUNDAY—FEBRUARY 6.

HOLD fast the form of sound words, which thou hast heard of me, in faith and love which is in Christ Jesus.

Timothy 1:13

MONDAY—FEBRUARY 7.

A WELL-KNOWN ego-boosting phrase reads: "Every day in every way I am getting better and better."

This is all very well and good, but I like this one better:

Good, better, best,
Never let it rest,
Till your good is better,
And your better best!

THE FRIENDSHIP BOOK

IT was a great blow when one of our neighbours was made redundant. His wife became very depressed because it seemed as if all their plans for settling in the area they loved so much had suddenly come to an end.

However, a job was offered in another town and the couple were all set to move. Yet Sue's heart was not in it. How could they leave the home they had put such work into, their many friends and the school where the children were so settled? Nevertheless, they did decide to move, and 12 months later she was able to write very happily to say how well everything had turned out. Work was going well, the children were happy, and Sue herself was so involved in new activities that the homesickness she had so much feared was quite short-lived.

We were all pleased that the story had ended so happily. Whenever I think of Sue, I am reminded of what Alexander Graham Bell wrote: "When one door closes, another opens, but we often look so long and so regretfully upon the closed door that we do not see the one that has opened for us."

PRECIOUS MOMENTS

EVEN as I stand here,
I see the day unfold,
I'd better get a move on,
Before it all grows old.
I'd better get a move on,
For time won't wait for me,
Each precious moment wasted,
Forever lost will be.

Phyllis Ellison.

THE FRIENDSHIP BOOK

MRS COTTON who lives in our road has been on her own for some years now and confesses that sometimes she doesn't sleep too well.

"It used to distress me at one time, Francis," she told me one day. "Now, though, instead of tossing restlessly I get up and look out of the window. Sometimes there is a light in the house opposite and I know that young Alan is burning the midnight oil with his studying. Often, too, I see a light in the house on the corner where there is someone who doesn't keep too well, and there is always a night-light in the Robinson twins' bedroom. Then, all at once the light goes on in Miss Brown's kitchen and I realise that she, too, is unable to sleep and has gone downstairs to make a cup of tea. Somehow, when I see those other lights, the night doesn't seem lonely any longer."

How very true — a little light often brings a great deal of comfort.

JENNIE lived in retirement on the south coast, having looked after her late brother who thought he had left his sister adequately provided for.

Unfortunately, inflation played havoc with the family savings, and Jennie began to realise that some cherished possessions would have to go, and she also moved from the family home into a little flat. Later, she told her minister that it was such a relief not to have to keep up appearances any longer.

"I have to live very simply," she said, "but somehow I have learned to appreciate small pleasures much more keenly."

It reminded me of something I once read: "It's not what we WANT — it's what we can do without that matters."

MICHAEL, a retired minister, had recently lost his wife. Ivy, a family friend and neighbour, was ill and housebound at the time, and knowing this, Michael went to visit her.

When Ivy found her old friend at the door she wondered what she could say to him to bring some comfort, but she need not have worried, for Michael was his usual courteous and cheerful self.

"I miss Ann very much and feel lonely," he confided to her, "but the faith that has helped me console others at times such as this, is now a help and comfort to me, and people are so kind."

In one of her lovely letters Ivy says that when he left she felt uplifted and, like Michael, was thankful for the strength of both faith and friendship.

SUNDAY—FEBRUARY 13.

BUT now being made free from sin, and become servants to God, ye have your fruit unto holiness, and the end everlasting life.

Romans 6:22

MONDAY—FEBRUARY 14.

A GERMAN friend told me recently about his nephew who had been staying with a family in Yorkshire. His English was reasonably good, but he kept referring to the jam on the table as marmalade.

Apparently, in German the word is the same for both.

However, the family and their guest were driving through Skipton when they saw a line of cars held up by the inevitable roadworks. "Look!" exclaimed their young visitor, "There's a traffic marmalade ahead."

B

THE FRIENDSHIP BOOK

THORA HIRD, one of our most popular entertainers, was born into a theatrical family, and spent almost a lifetime in the entertainment world from comedy to serious drama. More recently, of course, she presented favourite hymns in the BBC's "Praise Be!" series.

Shortly before her 80th birthday, she was interviewed by Terry Wogan on his chat show. Talking about appearances she said, "I often hear people say, 'I wish I looked like Marilyn Monroe', and I think how silly. I'm very ordinary looking and 'ordinary' is the loveliest word in the dictionary."

Abraham Lincoln, noted for his wise sayings, once said, "The Lord prefers common-looking people. That is why he makes so many of them."

So today, I salute all of us who are numbered amongst that vast throng of "ordinary looking" people — and are proud to be so!

MANY of us spend time worrying, not only in our waking hours, but also when we are asleep. We just cannot stop. As I hear about other people's problems day after day, I sometimes wonder if there are any non-worriers at all.

We worry about our work, our families, our money and our health, to name but a few common examples. We can make ourselves really ill or sometimes we try to pretend that the worry doesn't exist.

It's at times like these that we need a real friend. Someone who really does understand and who can share the strain or perhaps point out that there's nothing really to bother about. Sometimes a worry shared can be a worry gone.

THE FRIENDSHIP BOOK

R ECENTLY, the Lady of the House was looking back through her autograph book which she has kept since childhood. Some entries made her laugh, others gave kindly advice, and points to ponder.

"Listen to this, Francis," she said. "My mother's verse told me to 'Smile every day to bring cheer'. Grace, my friend, told me to 'Keep my head up and grow straight'. A school teacher advised me to 'Do my best now and always'.

"It's nice to read all these things again," she said. "They were all written a long time ago, but, you know, good advice never goes stale."

Of course she's absolutely right — as always!

O UR friend Sue has spent many years studying the Bible. She also has a great talent — perhaps derived from her extensive reading — for creating parables from her experiences of daily life. She is also a keen cyclist so, not surprisingly, she once told us that the more she rode her bike, the more she saw it as a "two-wheel parable".

"Take pot-holes, for example. Frequently I must alter course or risk being jarred or shaken, in order to avoid some hazard in the road — one which other road-users cannot see because they are farther away. I know they will wonder why I changed course. Life is like that. Jesus said, 'Judge not, that you be not judged.' "

Isn't that true? We rarely know what combination of pressures causes others to act the way they do. When bosses, colleagues, friends even, act in an unpredictable manner, we have to learn to make allowances, and accept them as they are.

THE people of Dent in the Pennines found they could earn a living by knitting. It meant a great deal of hard work — knitting all day and well into the night. Most of England had soon heard of "The Terrible Knitters of Dent" as Robert Southey, the poet, called them — terrible meaning "great", of course.

In fine weather they sat knitting on their doorsteps, or in groups on the flat tombstones of the churchyard. In Winter they would sit around the fire knitting to the rhythm of their special songs.

They knitted on their way to market and they knitted on their way to church — and even during the service. The parson didn't mind. He knew that all good things come from the combination of God's help and man's toil.

AND Paul dwelt two whole years in his own hired house, and received all that came in unto him.

Acts 28:30

RECENTLY, I caught sight of a poster. It read: "Poverty is what happens when people give up caring for one another!"

A friend happened to remark in this context: "In the help we give our neighbour God's will is done."

When I stopped to reflect, I realised that those who haven't many wordly goods often seem to be among the readiest to help each other. It reminded me of a Manx proverb: "When the poor help the poor, God laughs in approval."

THE FRIENDSHIP BOOK

HAVE you heard of florography? I must say that I hadn't until the Lady of the House told me about it.

Florography, it seems, is flower symbolism — a message said with flowers instead of words.

Every flower has its own message. Almond blossom, for example, says, "I am beginning to enjoy your friendship", rosemary says, "Your memory will never fade". So a mixed bouquet can speak volumes!

The Lady of the House loves flowers, especially wild ones, and points out that for centuries they have helped us. "Their perfumes have refreshed our homes, they have cured many an illness — and they also send their loving messages — so *we* really should care for *them!*"

Like the quiet, unassuming people of this world, flowers pass on their messages of strength and sweetness. They should never be overlooked, but always cherished.

AT the beginning of our church service recently, we sang one of my favourite hymns by Eleanor Farjeon:

Morning has broken, like the first morning,
Blackbird has spoken, like the first bird;
Praise for the singing, praise for the morning,
Praise for them springing, fresh from the Word.

It never fails to lift my heart in gratitude, for whatever happened yesterday, today is a new beginning and we have 24 hours of new time at our disposal.

Welcome to another new day!

THE FRIENDSHIP BOOK

I ONCE heard a radio presenter say that if we were feeling down, we should try to surround ourselves with bright things, the idea being that they would reflect their brightness and some of it would rub off on us.

It seems a good idea to seek something to lift our spirits — taking a walk in the park on a sunny day, inviting a cheerful friend round for a cup of coffee, or treating yourself to a bunch of flowers or some other small gift. Doing any of our favourite things can help a lot.

A family we know have a special game they save for long journeys. It's called WT, short for "wonderful things", and the object is to score points for each of the special things they pass — a field of new lambs, a bluebell wood, a village church or a rainbow. It keeps the journey from becoming monotonous and opens the travellers' eyes to the many beautiful things around them.

How about playing your own game of "wonderful things" wherever you happen to be today?

FRIDAY—FEBRUARY 25.

TREASURE

PARENTS are special, so guard them with care
Cherish and love them, whilst they are still there.
Cheer them and comfort their pains and their fears,
Help them and show them your thanks through
the years.
Give them your patience as they both grow old,
For the love you have shared, is more precious
than gold.

Chrissy Greenslade.

I READ once of a British engineer who, while serving abroad, was invited to a Kenyan's home for the week-end.

They spent some time sitting by a river, but then the visitor decided to display his swimming prowess by crossing to the far bank and back again. The local lads cheered and congratulated him, saying, "You must have magic skin."

"I don't think so," he replied. "It's no different to your coffee-coloured ones."

"But, it must be magic," they said. "If *we'd* swum across, we'd have been eaten by the crocodiles!"

N OW if we be dead with Christ, we believe that we shall also live with him.

Romans 6:8

O UR LORD came to give all that He had for the sake of mankind — yet of material things, He possessed very little. The following passage was sent to me by a friend from her church magazine. It is worth thinking about if ever we feel we are deprived of this world's goods.

"He was born in a borrowed stable; he taught from a borrowed boat; he fed 5,000 people with borrowed loaves and fishes; he borrowed the home of Martha and Mary to rest in; he rode into Jerusalem on a borrowed donkey; he celebrated the Last Supper in a borrowed room; he borrowed a stranger's strength to carry his cross and was finally buried in a borrowed tomb."

 MARCH

WHEN Sarah was only three she took ill and had to stay in bed. Her wealthy parents did their best to cheer her up with presents and surprises, but no matter how hard they tried, she showed no interest.

Then, one day a chaffinch alighted on to the window-sill. It stood there for a few moments, preening itself before flying off — but not before Sarah had seen it.

"Mummy, please put out some crumbs and it might come back," she pleaded.

Her mother did so, and from then on the chaffinch was a daily visitor. Sarah watched for it eagerly and from then on she began to make a rapid recovery. The colourful little bird did what expensive gifts had failed to do — gave her back the will to get better.

PERHAPS it is a sign of my age, or a streak of nostalgia, but I still find great pleasure in reading the old classics by authors such as Jane Austen, William Thackeray and a particular favourite, Charles Dickens. I have read some several times, and always see things in them that I missed before. Recently I read a comment by the writer Clifton Fadiman which put a slightly different interpretation on this observation:

"When you re-read a classic, you do not see more in the book than you did before; you see more in *you* than there was before."

A comforting thought — as a good book improves with age, so do our own personalities.

MAGIC

THERE is magic all around us,
If we only use our eyes.
There's enchantment in the Springtime,
In the fields and in the skies.
There's a blessing in the west wind
As it whispers in the trees,
There is healing in the sunlight
And the murmur of the seas.

There is magic in the morning
As we make another start,
There is kindness all about us,
And a smile can touch the heart.
There is music in our laughter
And it cheers a rainy day,
There is magic all around us—
Never let it slip away.

Iris Hesselden.

WE read lots of good advice about how to preserve our environment and many long and learned articles are written, full of dire warnings about the damage our modern ways of life do to our natural world.

However, whole volumes could not get the message across half so well as these words from the writer Hunter Davies. In the countryside, he said, we should:

"Take nothing but pictures; leave nothing but footprints; kill nothing but time."

That puts it all in a nutshell.

SATURDAY—MARCH 5.

WHAT a delight the crocuses in our garden are at this time of year — a lovely carpet of purple, gold and white. Last year's was the best display so far. When I first planted them some years back, there was not a lot to be seen for my efforts, just a few sparse clumps here and there. However, crocuses improve and increase as the years go by, and what may seem a disappointing showing in the first year or two soon becomes a rich Spring display.

They are like so many other things in life — be it creating a home, learning a new language or embarking on a project. Success is not achieved overnight and it often takes a long time before we can see and enjoy the fruits of our labours.

Let's never underestimate the importance of patience and perseverance — the crocuses know the secret.

SUNDAY—MARCH 6.

I WILL call on the Lord, who is worthy to be praised: so shall I be saved from mine enemies.

Samuel II 22:4

MONDAY—MARCH 7.

NEXT time someone is rude to you, and you feel like treating them the same way, remember this story of the great Buddha. When a man abused him he listened in silence, but when the man had finished, Buddha asked, "If a man declined to accept a present held out to him, to whom would it belong?" The man answered, "To him who offered it."

"My son," said Buddha, "I decline to accept your abuse, and request you to keep it for yourself."

THE FRIENDSHIP BOOK

THE Lady of the House and I recently went to say goodbye to an old friend, a beautiful horse chestnut tree in the park. It had been struck by lightning in a thunderstorm, and for safety's sake, the authorities decided it had to be cut down.

The horse chestnut has been part of the British landscape for less than 400 years, for it was introduced from the Balkans in 1616 as an ornamental tree for formal avenues. Now it grows freely in many parts of the country, producing lovely pink or white candles in Spring, umbrella-like leaves in Summer and horse chestnuts in Autumn.

Our special tree has been home to squirrels and wood pigeons; a source of nectar for bees; its canopy of branches has protected people from both rain and the hot midday sun; and it has been the setting for countless picnics and family conker expeditions.

Surely the tree is one of the best of Nature's gifts.

DAVID FROST, the TV presenter, once said, "If there's one thing I cannot abide, it's wasting time. Friends say that's rather puritanical of me, but I genuinely believe that, if there's one duty we all have, it's to use to the full whatever time or talents we may have been given."

Tubby Clayton, co-founder of Toc H, the charitable organisation for servicemen, used to say, "Service is the rent we pay for our room on earth", while George Bernard Shaw, noted for his trenchant observations, wrote, "A life spent in making mistakes is not only more honourable, but more useful than a life spent doing nothing."

Thoughts to keep in mind at the beginning of another new day!

THE FRIENDSHIP BOOK

THE Lady of the House and I decided to revive some of our memories of country rambles by returning to a once-familiar footpath. At first, the path was as we remembered it, well-worn and easy-going, but as we went on, the weeds grew taller, thistles crowded in, and stinging nettles and straggling brambles impeded our progress. More than once we thought of turning back.

Then, suddenly, we were out of the undergrowth. The path stretched ahead, winding between the trees.

We often wonder whether we've done the right thing, don't we? "Should we give up?" we ask ourselves when things begin to get difficult. But patience and persistence are always rewarded. The light at the end of the tunnel is always that much brighter for the effort we have made. William Fales expressed it thus:

And led by loving hands, and voice of love,
I swiftly scaled the mountainside above
The gloom and shadow, till the sunlit skies
Around me broke revealing Paradise.

FROM time to time a friend sends me her church's service sheet which often has a verse or message on it. Here is one about the importance of keeping Sunday special:

A Sabbath well spent
Brings a week of content
And strength for the toils of tomorrow.
But a Sabbath profaned
What so e'er may be gained
Is a certain forerunner of sorrow!

THE FRIENDSHIP BOOK

WE will always remember Amy. She was a widow with a family of four, and had a busy and often hard time when they were small, yet she was determined to give each one as much personal attention as she could.

Every week there was one evening set aside for a chat with one of them when they could discuss any worries or problems.

David's evening was always Wednesday. Years later, when he became a university lecturer, he wrote to his mother asking her to go on thinking of him on Wednesday evenings, saying that it would help him when "forming judgments".

She did as her son requested for the rest of her life, and Wednesday was always a special "Mother's Day" for David, a day when he felt strengthened and inspired by the knowledge that she was thinking of him and wishing him well.

IN every thing give thanks: for this is the will of God in Christ Jesus concerning you.
Thessalonians I 5:18

A FRIEND recently made this remark about a rather impulsive young man he works with: "I wish he'd put his brain in gear before he opens his mouth."

It's perhaps not quite as picturesque a comment as that of the Cumbrian villager who was overheard saying, "I always say that if you say what you think, you'd better think what you say."

A remark well worth bearing in mind.

TUESDAY—MARCH 15.

I KNOW a man whose life was changed by a poem. He had opened a business, but things were not going well, and he was on the point of giving up when he read the lines below. He decided to give it one more go — and has never looked back. May this poem help others, too:

When things go wrong as they sometimes will,
When the road you're trudging seems all uphill,
When funds are low and debts are high
And you want to smile, but you have to sigh,
When care is pressing down a bit,
Rest if you must, BUT DON'T YOU QUIT.

Success is failure turned inside out —
The silver tint of the clouds of doubt,
And you never can tell how close you are,
It may be near when it seems so far,
So, stick to the fight when you're hardest hit —
It's when things seem worst that
  YOU MUST NOT QUIT.

WEDNESDAY—MARCH 16.

HAVE you heard about the young man who went to the bank and asked to withdraw £100?

The cashier said, "I'm sorry, sir, you can't take that from your account because you haven't got that amount in it."

The young man went away, sadder but wiser.

It's only a story, but the moral is quite clear. If each day we fail to put a little into our bank account of life — our relationships, our leisure time, and even our ordinary everyday tasks — then we shouldn't be surprised if we get nothing out in return!

THE FRIENDSHIP BOOK

A READER sent me a delightful story which I'd like to pass on.

"Recently we had our two grandsons to stay with us while their mother was resting after the birth of a new baby. By seven o'clock each night they were bathed and in their pyjamas. This is when they liked to sit beside me looking at old photo albums before being tucked up in bed. They found pictures of themselves as babies, of their mummy when she was a little girl, and they were intrigued to find one of me on my wedding day.

" 'Granny,' said four-year-old James, scrutinising the lines on my face and my grey hair, 'you're not as pretty as you used to be.'

"Alex, who is older — and wiser — said, 'That's not important, James. It's what Granny's like inside that matters — and she's lovely.' And he gave me a hug."

Bless his heart!

O N a television gardening programme, we were shown a beautiful display of African violets, a mass of colour ranging from white through to palest pink, mauve, cerise and deepest purple — a breathtaking sight. They had been grown by a curate who runs an African violet centre.

He explained that they are very easy to propagate from their leaves — he simply puts the leaves back to back in pairs in a pot, so that they support one another. They very quickly take root and grow.

It's like life, isn't it? Take two people — in marriage, friendship, business or a charitable venture — and if they are wholeheartedly supporting one another, what splendid results there will be!

SPRING IS IN THE AIR

THE FRIENDSHIP BOOK

WE all make excuses — the Lady of the House says that I do this often! An excuse is usually made to avoid something that we do not want to do. Afterwards we often regret that we didn't face up to the situation, and then we feel guilty.

Many folk are often late for work, and maybe this reflects that they are afraid of what the day will bring. I recently read of someone writing a thesis on this subject. Their research found many of the usual excuses that we all make, and there were also some very odd ones. One man, as an excuse for being late for work, convinced his colleagues that a tube train in Central London had run over a cow!

When written down and recorded, most of these excuses were stupid and unreasonable. They show me that it is always wiser to be honest with friends and colleagues, admit our failures and weaknesses — and try to do better next time. No more excuses!

LET every soul be subject unto the higher powers. For there is no power but of God: the powers that be are ordained of God.

Romans 13:1

MY friend Ralph from Sheffield sent me a cutting from his evening paper. It concerned two young people of our acquaintance, and the report commented: "The couple were married on Friday, thus ending a friendship which began in their schooldays."

I hope it wasn't true . . .

THE FRIENDSHIP BOOK

OUR friend Sylvia was having problems with her teenage son, Jason. He was not a bad sort of boy. In fact, his teachers said he worked very hard, and at the shop where he had a Saturday job, he was well liked. Nevertheless, it seemed that when he was at home with his parents, there were always arguments.

"What can I do about it?" Sylvia asked her mother in despair.

"There are two things you can do nothing about," was the reply. "One is snow, the other is adolescence — but leave them alone and they'll both go away of their own accord."

Jason is now married with a young family of his own and when I met his mother last week, she was proudly telling me how well she gets on with them all. I'm sure that the days of teenage traumas have long been forgotten, even if the lessons from those days have been well learned.

A PROMINENT Methodist minister once told me that in one sense, preaching a sermon was easy.

"I wait for inspiration," he explained, "then I shut myself in my study, pray, think, arrange my headings, look for illustrations, and when I look at my congregation and have begun to deliver my text, the rest is easy."

However, he went on, "What I find really difficult is practising what I preach. Preaching is comparatively easy — living it out seven days a week is anything but. I do my best, though, and the grace of God helps me."

I found that comment, from a man who radiates Christian love, highly encouraging.

THE FRIENDSHIP BOOK

THERE are seats in a nearby shopping precinct. If the Lady of the House and I are feeling tired, we can sit down and rest awhile. We were relaxing there one day, when a shabbily-dressed gentleman with lots of shopping came and sat beside us. We chatted about this and that, then he told us that his name was Wilfred and mentioned in the course of conversation that he was an atheist. We parted on good terms and thought that our paths would never cross again.

A few weeks later, I found a picture of him in the local newspaper, and discovered why Wilfred had so much shopping. Some time previously, a poor, handicapped 80-year-old man was being evicted from his cottage home and was in despair. Wilfred, said the paper, was the widowed neighbour who had given up his home and bought one large enough for two. He now looks after his old friend with great kindness.

It isn't what we call ourselves that matters — it's what we *are* that counts.

I CAME across this charming little verse entitled "Friendship" recently. I have no idea who the author is, but the sentiments are well worth passing on.

It is my joy to find
*   At every turning of the road,*
The strong arms of a comrade kind,
*   To help me onward with my load;*
And since I have no gold to give,
*   And love alone must make amends,*
My daily prayer is while I live —
*   "God make me worthy of my friends."*

SATURDAY—MARCH 26.

I WENT sailing with a friend not long ago. He has always lived for the water, and now he is retired, scarcely a day passes but he is aboard his beloved boat. I was privileged then to be allowed to take the tiller. We were sailing along smoothly and I was pleased with my show of skill, while at the same time managing to listen intently to one of his many yarns. Suddenly, he stopped speaking, and then reminded me to watch my steering. "But the following wind is favourable!" I protested.

John smiled and nodded. "True," he said, "but that's when the danger of going off course is so great."

I have thought of his words many times since, for it is all too easy to veer off course when success or "smooth sailing" makes you satisfied and complacent. That kindly warning from a wise friend has often saved me from rushing off in the wrong direction.

SUNDAY—MARCH 27.

THEN Peter and the other apostles answered and said, We ought to obey God rather than men.

Acts 5:29

MONDAY—MARCH 28.

"WE'VE been having a geography quiz today, Mr Gay," said a passing schoolboy David when he spotted me in the garden. "Do *you* know where Felixstowe is?"

I was careful before I answered for I'm well aware of his little jokes: "It's at the end of Felix's foot," I said triumphantly.

"No — it's a port in Suffolk," said David with a glorious grin.

MAKING FRIENDS

TUESDAY—MARCH 29.

"OUR collection will be taken during the singing of the next hymn," the minister told his congregation.

One elderly lady rummaged in her handbag. She had left all her money at home except for a twenty pound note for emergencies, tucked away in the side of her bag. She felt very embarrassed and agitated. What was she to do?

When the collection plate reached her, she reluctantly put the note on top of the pile of coins.

Fortunately, the collector with the plate knew her well and guessed her predicament. He gently gave the note back to her. "You give enough every Sunday," he said. "And besides," he added with a cheeky grin, "God wants donations, not bribery!"

WEDNESDAY—MARCH 30.

DOWN with the letter "I"
I say,
Up with the letter "U",
Down with the phrase
"Let's not bother",
And up with the phrase
"Let's do!"

Anne Kreer.

THURSDAY—MARCH 31.

I WAS impressed by these questions sent by Mrs D. Robert of Guernsey. Read them — and you will find the answers in your heart:

How can you value each other, if you've never been parted; happiness, if you've never been sad; togetherness, if you've never been lonely; or love, if you've never loved?

APRIL

FRIDAY—APRIL 1.

EVERY day a slender, white-bearded elderly gentleman would set out in the late afternoon to post his letters. He always wore a hat and would raise it politely to friends and visitors when they said, "Good afternoon, Mr Shaw."

Bernard Shaw, the famous author, playwright and actor would spend several hours each day writing ten letters. They were to people whom he did not know, and perhaps would never meet. He received letters not just from budding authors asking for help, but from people seeking advice on such matters as life, marriage, children and careers.

Every day he would compose ten replies. Towards the end of his life, he jokingly told his friends tongue in cheek, "Just think how many more plays I could have written in the time I have spent writing letters every day!"

This story shows us that Bernard Shaw was a man who could not look on the needs of others without doing something to help.

SATURDAY—APRIL 2.

I HAVE long believed that gardening is good for you. Walking home the other evening and seeing some of our neighbours out mowing the grass, hoeing and raking, I was reminded of something I once read which has remained in my mind:

"Caring for a garden is like a parable of a gentle life, for he who sows courtesy, reaps friendship; and he who plants kindness, gathers love."

SUNDAY—APRIL 3.

THEN the same day at evening, being the first day of the week, when the doors were shut where the disciples were assembled for fear of the Jews, came Jesus and stood in the midst, and saith unto them, Peace be unto you.

John 20:19

MONDAY—APRIL 4.

YEARS ago in the USA there was a famous strain of wheat called Marquis. Millions of bushels were produced year after year, and it was claimed that it was the most prolific edible grain available, upon which millions depended. When this was said, it was also stated that 40 years previously you could have put all the Marquis Wheat in existence into one envelope. Such is the power of life that out of inauspicious beginnings, vital new foundations can be laid.

Jesus himself said, "Except a corn of wheat falls to the ground and dies, it remains only a single seed. But if it dies it produces many seeds." Therein lies the message of Easter — He died, and rose again showing the power of God to give new life. As a result, millions upon millions of people have found faith and hope and meaning in life.

TUESDAY—APRIL 5.

ARE you diffident about telling other folk your age? It perhaps depends how you are asked, but I don't think anything can beat the delightful Chinese way of showing respect to the elderly. They ask older people, "What is your glorious age?"

No wonder the answer can then be given with pride!

THE FRIENDSHIP BOOK

THE first glimpse of cowslips in Spring was always eagerly looked forward to when I was young, and I'm glad to say they can still be found today.

Last year, I was delighted to see a bed of cowslips growing in a very surprising place. One of the big grocery chains had opened a large store on the outskirts of a big town. The store lies below the level of the approach road, and the whole embankment, plus a large flowerbed at the entrance to the car park and petrol station, had been planted with cowslips.

Commerce isn't all counting the profits and saving on costs.

HOPE is a staff by which I may
Find strength to face another day,
A very faithful, loving friend,
Upon whose strength I can depend.

Hope is a comfort to my heart,
When other comforts all depart,
When stars no more in radiancy
Shine with the moon on you and me.

Hope is the Grace, which prompts me on,
When hope itself seems almost gone—
A little spur, to turn defeat,
Into a victory complete.

For, when all joy seemed well-nigh fled,
God gave the gift of hope instead,
A precious, kindly, living spark,
That pierces every kind of dark.

Margaret H. Dixon.

HAVE you noticed how many sayings there are connected with different parts of the body, all of which encourage us to keep going when things are difficult?

We are told to put our best foot forward; to dig our heels in; to keep our hand to the plough; to keep our chin up; to keep a stiff upper lip; to keep our nose to the grindstone, our eyes on the goal and our head held high.

Surely, if we follow all this good advice, we won't fail in our efforts "never to put a foot wrong"!

SATURDAY—APRIL 9.

JUST A MOMENT!

CAN you spare a moment
Throughout a busy day,
To chat to someone lonely
You meet upon your way?
So many folk are lonely,
And need a little care,
A word or two of comfort,
You could so easily spare.
And by your understanding,
The little things you've done,
You'll make the day much brighter,
And a far less lonely one.

Elizabeth Gozney.

SUNDAY—APRIL 10.

AND the disciples were filled with joy, and with the Holy Ghost.

Acts 13:52

THE FRIENDSHIP BOOK

MY neighbour John took his son, Paul, to see a football cup-tie.

Their team managed to beat their opponents from the other side of the river, much to everybody's surprise, for they'd always been unfortunate enough to lose in the past.

"That's answered my prayer, Daddy — I prayed that our team would win," said Paul afterwards.

"Supposing that a little boy on the other side had also prayed that *his* team might win — what then?" asked his father.

"Oh," replied Paul, aged six, "in that case it would have been a draw!"

AS I looked out of my window one stormy day and watched the trees rocking in the wind, I wondered how many birds would lose their nests that night.

It made me think of the storm petrel, or Mother Carey's Chicken as sailors once called it. When the sea is calm these birds can be seen apparently walking on the water, and it is said that the name "petrel" comes from the Bible story of St Peter walking across the water towards Jesus.

However, when the sea is rough, the petrels find shelter in the trough of the waves, avoiding the crest, and they will go ashore only if the storm is particularly furious or at breeding time, and then they make their nests and rear their young in the safety of a crevice in a rock or a disused burrow.

It's a striking example, I think, of the advantages of adaptability and being able to weather all the changing situations of life.

FLOWERS AND FEATHERS

THE FRIENDSHIP BOOK

ARE you keen on crosswords? The Lady of the House and I enjoy them immensely. Sometimes we are able to complete difficult crosswords fairly quickly, while at other times we don't even manage half of supposedly simpler ones. It all depends how quickly you interpret the clues.

In everyday life, people's personalities can present a bit of a puzzle to us, and how we interpret them will reflect on whether we think we can get on with them.

With a crossword there are often alternative words to sift through. Where people are concerned, we should try to reinterpret first impressions and the way we describe them.

Instead of stand-offish, the word shy may be more appropriate, insecure instead of domineering, lonely rather than over-talkative. Once we have solved the clues to people's true personalities, we will often be very pleasantly surprised indeed.

"I MUST write and tell you this," explained a friend from Yorkshire. "We hear so much nowadays about the difficulties faced by teachers — lack of discipline among pupils, their unwillingness to learn and so on. It is good, however, to hear the other side; there are classroom joys, too."

This had been brought home to him when he attended a concert at his granddaughter's school. At the end of a most enjoyable evening, the Head Teacher thanked the parents and friends for coming along. To round it all off, he said these words which my friend found very moving:

"Thank you for *lending* us your children."

What a lovely thing to say and for parents to hear!

FRIDAY—APRIL 15.

TODAY I would like to share some more jottings from my notebook on the subject of prayer.

"Prayer should be your steering wheel — not your spare wheel."

"If you can't sleep, don't count sheep — talk to the Shepherd."

"I've lived long enough to be thankful God didn't give me all I asked for."

"If you are suffering from a long-standing, deep-seated trouble — try kneeling."

"Lord, when we are wrong, make us willing to change, and when we are right, make us easy to live with."

I hope you'll find these points to ponder as helpful as I do.

SATURDAY—APRIL 16.

WANT to send a friend a message of goodwill? I can think of no better way to do it than to quote these lovely lines by Iris Hesselden:

I wish you serendipity,
A little magic in your life,
And gentle, calm serenity,
To combat stress and strife.

I wish you sweet tranquillity,
Along your future way,
And love to grow abundantly,
To fill your world each day.

SUNDAY—APRIL 17.

THERE is none holy as the Lord: for there is none beside thee: neither is there any rock like our God.

Samuel I 2:2

THE FRIENDSHIP BOOK

I WONDER what comes into your mind when you think of the word "home"? Is it the town where you were born, the place you spent your childhood, the house shared with a loved one, or some other place where you experienced your greatest happiness?

I have been reading about a lady who was unhappy at the prospect of being moved to another old people's home. Her comment was, "It's not got a homely atmosphere like here. We've got two cats and a coal fire, and staff who care about us. What more could you want?"

That old lady, I think, had recognised the true essence of a home — the place where we can be ourselves, comfortable, relaxed, at ease, in our own armchair with our favourite possessions around us — in fact, truly "at home".

As Jane Austen wrote in "Northanger Abbey", "Wherever you are, you should always be contented, but especially at home, because there you must spend the most of your time."

HAVE you noticed how often colours figure in our speech? We talk of somebody in a black mood, a brown study, or being green with envy. Sometimes we admit to feeling blue. Then there are red letter days, golden handshakes and clouds with a silver lining!

Today, I'll think about the many coloured things that have pleasant associations for me — red slippers and crimson roses; the full moon and ripening corn fields; rosy cheeks and strawberry ice-cream; trees in Springtime and a well-kept lawn; tangerines and home-made marmalade; violets and pansies; a Summer sky and a bluebell wood.

What a beautiful world it is!

APPLE BLOSSOM TIME

D

THE FRIENDSHIP BOOK

BLESSINGS

*B*LESS me, Lord, along the way,
As I begin another day;
Bless my eyes, that they may see
The beauty that's surrounding me.
Bless my feet, that they may tread
With courage, on the road ahead,
Bless all the people that I love,
And give them guidance from above,
Not least of all, I pray you'll bless
All those who suffer loneliness.
I thank thee, Lord, in fervent prayer
For all thy blessings, everywhere.

Dorothy M. Loughran.

IN a sudden burst of energy I decided to move a couple of uneven slabs on our garden path. When I lifted them, I discovered a great colony of ants scurrying around busily.

What fascinated me, though, was the speed with which they moved to protect their community at a time of danger. An army of mature ants marched in and carried hundreds of eggs to a safe place, and when I returned ten minutes later to inspect the scene, there was not one egg to be seen — just one or two scouts patrolling the area.

What a lesson we can learn from the ants! One person alone cannot accomplish a great deal, but teamwork and co-operation can.

It brought to mind something I heard on the radio. "God said, 'I gave you the world and everything in it.' And the man said, 'But we need help.' God replied, 'That is why I gave you each other.' "

THE FRIENDSHIP BOOK

THE Lady of the House always says that if she took away all my "imaginary worries", I'd still find *something* to bother me. That's why this verse by Phyllis Ellison is especially appropriate.

Felt a bit worried this morning,
For I awoke with no worries at all,
So I've spent all the day quietly worrying,
What it is that I cannot recall.

"I HATE the phrase 'physically handicapped'," said Ronnie West, one of the sufferers from the horrific effects of Thalidomide. "We physically different people can do almost anything given the right motivation," he added.

He has proved the truth of this in many fields, from the academic to the sports arena — he has competed successfully in the Disabled Olympics.

His reaction is no isolated one. Such young men and women can be called "plus people". They contribute so much in so many walks of life that their achievements seem amazing to those of us blessed with good health and no disabilities.

Such high achievers under adversity do not want us to be sorry for them. All they ask is that we should accept them as we do anyone else, and give them every opportunity to prove their worth in the world. And how wonderfully they respond!

NOW the God of peace be with you all. Amen.

Romans 15:33

THE FRIENDSHIP BOOK

THE 23rd Psalm is a favourite with many preachers and congregations alike.

One little girl learning the Psalm kept getting it wrong. She came out with, "The Lord is my Shepherd, that's all I want." The preacher who told me this story suggested that perhaps she was more correct than she realised!

Another preacher in Cornwall was emphasising the defencelessness of the sheep. "What could it do to protect itself?" he asked his flock.

Quick as a flash came the answer from a country girl sitting in front of him, "He can butt. Our old ram knocked down Grandfather the other day."

DRIVING past the Methodist Church in the little market town of Knaresborough in Yorkshire, I was intrigued to find that it was situated in Gracious Street. With a name like that to live up to, it must be both a challenge and an encouragement to the residents and those who worship there, for the way we feel about certain places usually influences the way we think and behave.

My dictionary defines "gracious" as "characterised by or showing kindness and courtesy; merciful or compassionate". All the good things, in fact, that St Paul wrote of to the Church in Phillipi: ". . . whatsoever things are pure, whatsoever things are lovely, whatsoever things are of good report; if there be any virtue, and if there be any praise, think on these things." Good advice indeed.

So, if we are fortunate enough to be living in "Gracious Street" — whatever other name it may happen to go by — let's be sure that we treat it with the respect it deserves!

THE FRIENDSHIP BOOK

H ERE are some lines translated from Sanskrit which seem to have a message for us all.

Yesterday is but a dream
And tomorrow only a vision,
But today well lived makes
Every yesterday a dream of happiness
And every tomorrow a vision of hope.

On the same theme, actor Tommy Steele once said, "Every night I just look forward to waking up tomorrow and enjoying another day's work."

Truly, words to encourage us!

O LD people can be very "down to earth" about their views on life. When the actress Gwen Ffrangcon-Davies was interviewed at the age of 97 on the BBC programme "Omnibus", she was asked if the prospect of death worried her. Her reply was, "No, but doing anything for the first time *does* make me nervous."

Somebody else once observed: "I find that with the passing years my pace is just a little slowed; I may not go so fast or far — but I see more along the road."

Serenity is one of the things that often increases as we go through life. It comes as one of the compensations of growing older and learning the lesson of courage to fight for what can be remedied, fortitude to bear what cannot be taken away, and wisdom to know the difference.

However difficult the path, we can all take comfort in the knowledge that the good, the true and the beautiful in life endure for ever.

THE FRIENDSHIP BOOK

EVELYN WOODLEY often sends me a few lines which speak volumes. Here are three examples:

> The word race is found in "Grace";
> May "Grace" be in every "Race".

> Be truthful in what you mean to say,
> But, don't be mean in the way you say it!

> Think a little,
> Try a little.
> Achieve more than a little.

MANY years ago Fay Inchfawn wrote books of verse which were very popular because of their happy faith and outlook. It was said that "if Fay Inchfawn cannot bring some compensation to you in your humdrum daily toil — well, nobody can!"

Here's an extract from her poem "The Good Samaritan" — as topical today as when it was first written:

> *She knocked so gently that I had not heard.*
> *So in she came, with just a cheery word,*
> *And as she talked she started washing up.*
> *She coaxed me to sit down . . .*

> *She fetched up groceries from the town,*
> *And got the tea — kind Mrs Brown!*
> *She washed the children, and she said*
> *She'd love to put them all to bed.*

> *At last when everything was right,*
> *She found her hat and said "Goodnight."*

MAY

SUNDAY—MAY 1.

AND whatsoever ye do in word or deed, do all in the name of the Lord Jesus, giving thanks to God and the Father by him.

Colossians 3:17

MONDAY—MAY 2.

I LIKE the note recorded in a magazine 100 years ago, concerning the Rev. Hugh Price Hughes, M.A., a popular Wesleyan Methodist preacher of that time It seems that the steward of a little country church used to read his name to his congregation as, "The Reverend Hug Price Hug his Ma!"

TUESDAY—MAY 3.

THERE is an old story that, as Joseph, Mary and the Baby Jesus fled to Egypt, pursued by Herod's soldiers, they stopped to speak to a farmer who had just ploughed his field before sowing seed. To the farmer's surprise, the Baby began to speak and told him to have his harvesting tools ready for use that very afternoon. The Babe also said that, when the pursuing soldiers asked if he had seen them, the farmer was to say that they had passed when he was sowing the grain.

It all happened as predicted. The soldiers came along that afternoon, and when they questioned the farmer he was able to say, quite truthfully, that the people they were seeking had indeed passed that way, when he was planting the seed he was now harvesting.

"That must have been months ago," said the soldiers, turning to go in another direction, and thus the Holy Family finished their journey in safety.

THE FORCE OF NATURE

THE FRIENDSHIP BOOK

WEDNESDAY—MAY 4.

I AM always pleased to see the first lilies of the valley nodding their heads in our garden, for I know how much the Lady of the House likes to pick a small bunch to grace our living-room table.

It is one of the oldest of flowers and is said to have been cultivated in gardens for more than 400 years. Legend tells us that it lures the nightingale by its scent and leads him to his mate.

Sometimes it is known as "Our Lady's Tears" because it was said that the delicate white flower was formed by the tears shed by the Virgin Mary at the foot of the Cross. Another name for it is "Ladder to Heaven" because the tiny flower bells grow like steps up the stem. It has associations with the second coming of Christ and monks used to grow it to decorate altars. The French call it "Muguet de Mai" and like to wear it as a buttonhole to celebrate May Day.

In flower language the lily of the valley is called "return of happiness", so with its fragile, pure white bells, sweet fragrance and the belief that it has the power of pointing man's thoughts to a better world, it is not surprising that modern brides still choose to include a sprig or two in their wedding bouquet.

THURSDAY—MAY 5.

ONE thing that matters most of all
Is do you whine or grin,
Are you a gallant cheery soul
Refusing to give in?
A bit of pluck, a smile, a song,
Will see you through when things go wrong.

Barbara Jemison.

THE FRIENDSHIP BOOK

WE have an elderly friend, Jane, who is a great philosopher in her own quiet way. Recently we called on her, and the Lady of the House found her sitting in front of her dressing-table mirror.

"Getting ready to go out, Jane?" she asked.

"No," Jane replied. "I've just been sitting here 'counting my blessings'. It's surprising what a lot of things we have to be thankful for," she added, "and just now I'm thinking how nice it is that wrinkles don't hurt!"

"CHARITY begins at home" is a saying with which most of us are familiar, but have you heard the words, "Charity that begins at home, stays at home"?

I was reminded of them when our Christian Aid envelope was popped through the letterbox one May morning appealing for money to improve health care, agriculture, education and training, and to provide emergency relief for the poorest of the world's poor.

We may often feel that we have enough calls on our pocket, but how can we resist an appeal that tells us for example that £1 will buy vaccinations for 30 Indian children against measles, whooping cough and diphtheria; or that £3 will buy six trees to prevent soil erosion and drought?

Every little helps. I read that one collector was handed six duck eggs instead of money. Not to be deterred, she looked up her recipe for a rich Christmas cake, baked the cake, auctioned it, and sent the proceeds as part of her Christian Aid collection.

So when that friendly Christian Aid lady knocks on my door, I'm determined not to let my charity "stay at home".

THE FRIENDSHIP BOOK

AND this is the record, that God hath given to us eternal life, and this life is in his Son.

John I 5:11

IN THIS BUSY WORLD

IN this busy world, we may
Forget to pass the time of day;
Small courtesies are so worthwhile
When accompanied with a smile.
Each and every little thing
Pleasant satisfaction bring:
"Excuse me" — "Thank you" —
"Sorry" — "Please" —
What simpler words are there than these?

Dorothy M. Loughran.

RECENTLY, the Lady of the House was reading that fascinating novel "The Bishop's Mantle" by Agnes Sligh Turnbull, and she drew my attention to Aunt Samantha.

A country girl, she was married to the Rev. Samuel Adams, the assistant minister at St Matthew's. Her command of language wasn't very good, but everyone loved her all the same.

"You like people, don't you?" someone once asked her.

"Oh, my, yes! As I always say, the Lord never made a person I couldn't take to my heart if I had to."

I think Aunt Samantha had discovered the secret of living in harmony with others, don't you?

OUR WORLD

THE FRIENDSHIP BOOK

A YOUNG man we know is a very keen gardener. His plot is not very big, but is full of lovingly tended plants, and callers rarely depart without a buttonhole or generous gift of fruit or vegetables. He told me recently that he likes getting visitors, but there's one he dreads to see dropping in.

"I know he's an expert on gardening," he said, "but his visits always leave me feeling depressed. You see, he always manages to notice some weeds that I've overlooked."

On my way home, I mulled over those words. Wouldn't the world seem a more beautiful place if we all took more notice of the flowers, and a lot less of the weeds?

O NE of our friends had been holidaying in Nova Scotia and came home very enthusiastic about the friendliness of the people there and the caring attitude of the community. He was surprised to find it was quite safe to leave houses unlocked whilst the owner was out.

The thing that impressed him most, though, was that at intervals on each road leading from schools, certain houses displayed a special card in the window. On making enquiries, he found that the resident was an approved volunteer; children finding themselves in any kind of trouble on the way home could call at one of these houses and be comforted, bandaged up, or whatever was necessary, until a parent was available to take them home again.

It's one of those nice "Good Neighbour" schemes that do so much to foster the community spirit — wherever it may be!

THE FRIENDSHIP BOOK

OLD Fred is now mostly housebound because of his arthritis. He struggles bravely to keep his small home clean and tidy, and especially enjoys folk dropping in for a chat. The last time we visited him, he pointed to a verse on his wall.

"That," he said, "could have been written for me."

The lines ran:—

When life's made up of little things,
The humdrum tasks that each day brings,
When every job needs lots of grit
Before you can accomplish it —
A daily dose of courage take,
Another cheerful effort make.
Resolve to finish what's begun,
Then every day's a battle won!

RECENTLY I had the pleasure of attending the christening of the newest baby in our family. It was a very happy occasion and, after the service, family and friends were invited to a buffet lunch at the baby's home to celebrate this special event. What an enjoyable time it was as family friendships separated by time and miles were renewed.

It's good to have occasions when we can have a special celebration with those we love. Weddings, anniversaries and birthdays are opportunities that immediately come to mind, but what about less obvious events — examination successes, retirement, moving into a new house, or the successful completion of some neighbourhood project?

Let's not neglect any excuse to make the most of any special event that comes along. Life is what we make it!

THE FRIENDSHIP BOOK

BLESSED are ye that hunger now: for ye shall be filled. Blessed are ye that weep now: for ye shall laugh.

Luke 6:21

THE very nicest folk, I think,
Are not the stars who shine
So brightly in the public eye —
The clever folk who sign
Big contracts, hit the headlines and
Snatch fortunes from a languid hand.
The very nicest folk are just
The friendly folk you meet
Most anywhere, the folk you're glad
To talk to in the street;
The folk you tell your worries to
Because you know they're fond of you.

I KNOW we have to consider the serious and the solemn as we go through life, but has it ever occurred to you that it would be foolish to take life so solemnly that we stop enjoying life's pleasures — the opportunity to fall in love, to enjoy friendships, to help others, to smell a rose . . .

Perhaps Oscar Hammerstein, the lyricist of that enchanting musical "Oklahoma!", expressed it more succinctly: "I know the world is filled with troubles and many injustices, but reality is as beautiful as it is ugly. I think it is just as important to sing about 'beautiful mornings' as it is to talk about slums. I just couldn't write anything without hope in it."

F

THE FRIENDSHIP BOOK

WEDNESDAY—MAY 18.

TIME is so precious that it should never be frittered away. The strange thing is that when time *is* wasted this happens not in hours, but in odd minutes, and they soon add up to make a surprisingly large total. After all, a bucket with a small hole in the bottom gets just as empty as a bucket that is deliberately kicked over!

That's why I've resolved to waste as little time as possible — every moment is precious, and it is surprising how much can be achieved when the clock seems against us.

THURSDAY—MAY 19.

A PRISON is a most unlikely institution to exhibit at the Chelsea Flower Show, but that is exactly what Leyhill Open Prison did, becoming the first jail to feature at the famous event.

Gardening is one of the rehabilitation projects at Leyhill, and a group of prisoners was encouraged to enter — with only six weeks to meet the deadline.

Their chosen theme of 40 colourful herbs, vegetables and fruits, designed in three circles, expressed the feelings and emotions of the different stages of prison life translated into gardening terms. The first circle bordered by Dartmoor granite contained prickly and thorny plants symbolising the harshness and hardness in coming to terms with a prison sentence. The second one, surrounded by softer Portland stone, was filled with mellow plants and crops to show hope, while the final circle contained sweet fruits and spreading strawberries to express freedom and a better life outside.

This edible garden was awarded the silver gilt medal of the Royal Horticultural Society.

THE FRIENDSHIP BOOK

CHILDREN often have a gentle logic that helps us all to see life in a wider perspective. I like the story of the little girl who returned home after visiting her grandmother who was in hospital for a knee operation.

"How's Granny?" asked her father.

"Oh, she's fine," the little girl replied. "It's only her leg that's not too good."

I HAVE been dipping into some of Fay Inchfawn's verses and came on these thoughtful lines:

> *You have a famous cook, 'tis true,*
> *Your ménage is the best,*
> *You are a splendid hostess, too,*
> *And such an ideal guest.*
> *But, can you eat of humble pie*
> *A truly generous slice,*
> *Without one soft, regretful sigh,*
> *As if it tasted nice?*
>
> *You can from any instrument*
> *Draw music sweet and clear.*
> *Like Orpheus, 'tis your gay intent*
> *To soothe and charm the ear.*
> *Harp — viol — 'cello — all of these*
> *Your servants! Let me see?*
> *Can you play second fiddle, please,*
> *And make a melody?*

TO the only wise God our Saviour, be glory and majesty, dominion and power, both now and ever. Amen.

Jude 1:25

THE FRIENDSHIP BOOK

DO you watch television quiz programmes? I must admit I sometimes pit my wits against all the clever people who take part in them.

The Lady of the House came in when I was watching one recently. She sat for a few moments in silence and then she said, "These games are all very well, but surely life itself is the most fascinating game of all. Each day it presents us with a new opportunity, a new idea, or a new problem. Of course, we don't know all the answers in life — we never will. That's what makes it so exciting!"

Of course she's right.

I'M glad I kept my autograph album. It's full of happy memories of the past — of aunts and uncles, teachers, schoolboy idols and chums who all left their marks on it. Here's a verse from my collection which I re-read recently:

It was only a sunny smile,
And little it cost in the giving,
But it scattered the night like the morning light,
And made my day worth living.

That's a sentiment that will surely go on being true for ever.

MARGARET, a middle-aged friend, was feeling rather pleased with herself when we met her returning from the shops.

"I was at the chemist's," she said, "and I didn't want all the customers to know my business so I whispered to him, 'Have you anything for grey hair?' He whispered back, 'Yes — the greatest respect!' "

VALE OF PEACE

THE FRIENDSHIP BOOK

*A*S long as I can walk one step,
    I'll walk, dear Lord, with you.
As long as I can hear one word,
    I'll listen, Lord, to you.
As long as I can clasp my hands,
    I'll clasp them both in prayer.
As long as I am here, dear Lord,
    I'll know that you are there.

                            Jean Harris.

FRIDAY—MAY 27.

QUOTATIONS from the writings and speeches of Abraham Lincoln are legion, but I came across one the other day which was new to me and which we might well remember:

"Die when I may I want it said of me that I plucked a weed and planted a flower wherever I thought a flower would grow."

I'm sure he was not just thinking of the weeds and flowers which grow in our gardens!

SATURDAY—MAY 28.

I HAVE been reading that mountain goats have what appears to be a great deal of commonsense. If two of them meet on a narrow rocky ledge where it would be impossible to pass, and dangerous even to turn back, one of the goats will lie down and allow the other to walk over it.

What a sensible thing to do and what a lesson for us all! Many a relationship has been spoiled by wanting our own way all the time, or by refusing to swallow our pride and admit we have been wrong. It's better to lose an argument than a friendship. Yes, these goats know a thing or two!

SUNDAY—MAY 29.

HOLDING forth the world of life; that I may rejoice in the day of Christ, that I have not run in vain, neither laboured in vain.

Philippians 2:16

MONDAY—MAY 30.

I HAVE been interested in what Dr Harry Emerson Fosdick, Bible teacher and minister of a well-known church in New York, once said about water.

Comparing the Sea of Galilee and the Dead Sea, he said that both consist of the same water, but whilst the Sea of Galilee is alive and sparkling, the Dead Sea is unhealthy. The reason, he explains, is that the Sea of Galilee has an outlet. It gathers in its riches so that it can pour out its waters again to fertilise the whole of the Jordan Plain. On the other hand, the Dead Sea has no outlet and never gives away its waters. Being highly saline, and hoarding all that comes into it, it can support no life.

What a gloomy prospect for living it would be if we kept all that we had and none of us ever gave anything away! So here's to the many things we *can* share with others — friendship, time, kindness, sympathy and love.

TUESDAY—MAY 31.

I HAVE never liked the sound of the old expression about "keeping your nose to the grindstone", but I do see the point of a rather similar saying which I heard for the first time recently:

"Life is a grindstone. Whether it grinds you down or polishes you up depends entirely upon the stuff you're made of."

JUNE

WEDNESDAY—JUNE 1.

A S I waited at the newsagent's counter to pay for our papers, I overheard a lady remark as she bought a very attractive card, "Yes, it's for my daughter. It's her birthday tomorrow."

"Is it a special one?" enquired the assistant.

"Not really," came the reply. Then the customer corrected herself and said, "Well, I suppose *every* birthday is special, isn't it?"

Indeed it is. Whether a child's first birthday, a young person on the threshold of adulthood, or someone who has achieved three-score years and ten, each birthday is of special significance and unique to the person concerned.

One family I know has four children, and few days pass without a little squabble between one or other. However, their mother has made it a rule that when someone has a birthday, everybody is nice for the whole of the day to the one celebrating the special day.

It's a lovely idea, and wouldn't it be nice if it spread to include every day of the year?

THURSDAY—JUNE 2.

"I 'VE got a new riddle for you today," said my young neighbour when he spotted me over the garden fence. "What were the four men doing at the barbecue?"

"Oh, I expect they were having a meal cooked in the open air," I replied, knowing full well that I was not going to be right.

"No, they were waiting at the barber's for a haircut!"

HERE is an anonymous verse which I copied into my notebook some time ago. I'd like to share it with you today:

A truth that stands out sharp
And clear as cloudless day:
God cannot answer prayers
That people do not pray!

It is a reminder that, like many other things in life, progress can be made only when we ourselves make the first move!

SATURDAY—JUNE 4.

I WAS asked to help on the white elephant stall at our annual church garden party, and amongst the hotch-potch of articles was a rather garish mug bearing the words: *SMILE — life is as good as you make it.*

It wasn't long before it was carried off triumphantly by a small boy as a present for his mother. Although I found the mug quite unattractive, I liked the motto, for it reminded me that whatever happens in life, it is the way we react that is important. We can remember the rain, the hard times, the unkind things said to us — or we can remember.the sunshine, the answered prayers and our many blessings.

As a wise old gardener once said, "Some folk grumble because God put thorns on the roses, but I think it's better to thank Him for putting roses on the thorns."

SUNDAY—JUNE 5.

BUT he that is joined unto the Lord is one spirit.

Corinthians I 6:17

THE FRIENDSHIP BOOK

THE Lady of the House and I were entertaining an old friend at home recently. The time passed quickly as we exchanged reminiscences and brought ourselves up to date with news.

"Doesn't time fly when you're having fun!" smiled our friend as he left. He'd been like a breath of fresh air, and to say that we missed him the next day would be the understatement of the year. George Birdseye put it this way:

> The longest day is in June, they say,
>   The shortest in December.
> They did not come to me that way;
>   The shortest I remember—
> You came a day with me to stay,
>   And filled my heart with laughter;
> The longest day — you were away —
>   The very next day after.

JOHN WESLEY, it was said, had a dream that he went to the Heavenly Gates and found they were shut. He called out, "Are there any Methodists in there?"

The answer came back, "No."

He called out again, "Are there any Baptists in there?"

"No," was the reply.

"Any members of the Church of Scotland?"

"No."

"Any United Reformed Church members?"

"No."

"Well, then," he called out, "who *is* in there?"

Back came the answer, "We are all Christians!"

THE FRIENDSHIP BOOK

IN 1679 an 18-year-old youth called Nicholas left his family in Nottinghamshire to go to London to be a draughtsman for Sir Christopher Wren. He found himself involved with all the important buildings of the time, including St Paul's Cathedral.

Nicholas Hawksmoor became England's first professional architect and was appointed to build 50 new churches in London. Yet, in spite of his fame he was a modest man and did not move in high social circles.

His letters show that he had a healthy respect for his stonemasons and craftsmen. Such was his concern for his workers' families, that he would often give them paternal advice. He would watch their children grow up, and when they were ill would suggest what remedies they should take. As they grew up, he saw that they were all placed in suitable jobs.

Nicholas Hawksmoor was not only the architect of beautiful buildings but the architect of a very fine and generous character — one still to be admired today.

WHEN I visited our old friend Mary recently, she confessed that the thumb of her left hand had been giving her quite a lot of pain. It was the result of an old injury that had been neglected and had left her with a misshapen joint.

"But, do you know," she said, "one of my taps is so stiff that I can't turn it at all with my right hand, but with this funny old left one I can turn it quite easily. It's odd," she added, "how something good can come out of something bad."

There is always something to be thankful for in every situation, isn't there?

MY gardening friend called round this morning to ask if I would like a tray or two of surplus Summer bedding plants.

"They're not star performers such as dahlias and delphiniums," he said, "but you will find them useful to plant here and there amongst the more spectacular flowers. They will act as a foil for them and will settle happily in any odd corner."

So I accepted gratefully and spent a happy hour planting them. Now I look forward to seeing them blooming and brightening the uninteresting spots in our garden.

Those plants are rather like life, I feel. We can't all be "star performers", nor would we wish to be. How very valuable are those people who can adapt to fit in with others — and what a funny old world it would be if there was nobody willing to play second fiddle!

SATURDAY—JUNE 11.

A FIVE-YEAR-OLD girl prayed, "Dear Lord, please try to put vitamins and good things in sweets and ice-cream and not just in spinach and cod liver oil."

A little boy, repeating the Lord's Prayer, altered it to "Give us this day our daily oranges."

When gently corrected and told it should be "daily bread", he replied, "No, I've got plenty of bread, what I want is oranges!"

SUNDAY—JUNE 12.

GRACE be with all them that love our Lord Jesus Christ in sincerity. Amen.

Ephesians 6:24

THE FRIENDSHIP BOOK

THERE'S a story about a lady in distress who went to see her minister, and, encouraged by his sympathetic manner, she poured out all her troubles.

At last she stood up, smiling. "I feel so much better now," she said. "Thank you very much for all your help and advice."

The minister bade her goodbye, without ever having spoken a word.

I am reminded of something written many years ago: "No medicine is more valuable, none more efficacious, none better suited to the cure of all our temporal ills than a friend to whom we may turn for consolation in times of trouble and with whom we may share our happiness in times of joy."

A FEW weeks ago I came across this ancient and very beautiful Sioux Indian prayer. What a lot of wisdom it contains! :

"Oh, Great Spirit, whose voice I hear in the winds, whose breath gives life to the world, hear me. I am small and weak. I need your strength and wisdom. May I walk in beauty. May my eyes ever behold the red and purple sunset. Make my hands respect the things you have made, and my ears sharp to your voice.

"Make me wise so that I may know the things you have taught your children, the lessons you have hidden in every leaf and rock.

"Make me strong not to be superior to my brothers and sisters but to be able to fight my greatest enemy, myself. Make me ever ready to come to you with straight eyes so that when life fades as the fading sunset, my spirit will come to you without shame."

THE FRIENDSHIP BOOK

A GARDENER'S NIGHTMARE

THE azaleas are all failures,
*   And the dahlias are the same.*
Each lily's willy-nilly,
*   Looking silly — such a shame.*

Each aster's a disaster,
*   Each cotoneaster, too.*
Morning glory tells a story
*   That's so moribund and blue.*

Each poppy is so sloppy
*   In the floppiest display.*
Each lupin has been droopin'
*   In the most stupendous way.*

The escallonia and begonia
*   Look forlorn and very drear.*
The camellia and lobelia
*   Just can't conceal a tear.*

The gardener wakened with a start,
*   Then assessed his nightmare viewing:*
"It serves me right for dosing off,
*   When I should be up and doing!"*

                    J.M. Robertson.

I LIKE this little bon mot I came across the other day, and I'm sure you will, too:
"An optimist may be wrong just as often as a pessimist — but he has more fun."
How true!

SOMEWHERE, SOMEONE

SOMEWHERE, someone is waiting
For a kindly word or two,
Just anticipating
Greetings warm and true;
Events and news need sharing
By letter or by phone
To show that someone's caring
For those who live alone.

Dorothy M. Loughran.

SATURDAY—JUNE 18.

IN the 1930s there was great poverty in London's East End. Two schoolmistresses at Hoxton were upset when they realised that the children hadn't any toys, and they thought up a scheme. They appealed for farthings and collected enough to buy toys to fill home-made bags to give to the children each year.

Demand always exceeded the supply, so only the small children were lucky enough to receive a Farthing Bag. In order that it would be done fairly, each child was measured under an arched gateway in Hoxton. If they could stand upright under it, they were eligible for a bag!

These modest gifts, bought with the humble farthings, brought sunshine into otherwise bleak childhoods.

SUNDAY—JUNE 19.

I AM Alpha and Omega, the beginning and the ending, saith the Lord, which is, and which was, and which is to come, the Almighty.

Revelation 1:8

F

THE FRIENDSHIP BOOK

IN a competition on the theme of international friendship, a shop in Exeter displayed this poster which won one of the prizes:

Don't walk in front of me,
I may not follow.
Don't walk behind me,
I may not lead.
Just walk beside me
And be my friend.

TODAY is the 21st June, the Summer solstice, when daylight hours are at their maximum and days are at their loveliest. An old country saying tells us that "Mist in May and heat in June, bring all things into tune."

In the old Roman calendar June was the fourth month of the year and it is thought that it was named in honour of the goddess Juno. It is the month when wild flowers fill the hedgerows and honeysuckle scents the evening air, when gardens come into their midsummer glory, the cuckoo changes its tune and the elder displays its creamy white clusters of blossom which are said to announce the ·true arrival of Summer.

The poet Jean Ingelow captures the feeling of a June day beautifully:

Crowds of bees are busy with clover,
Crowds of grasshoppers skip at our feet,
Crowds of larks at their matins hang over,
Thanking the Lord for a life so sweet.

So today, I, too, will take time to be especially grateful for all that this Summer's day promises.

THE FRIENDSHIP BOOK

HERE are some words of wisdom from the football pitch:

"The trouble with never having a goal in your life is that you can spend the whole of it running up and down the field and never scoring."

FORTY years ago a Christian pastor, blinded during wartime training exercises as an army chaplain, gave a memorable talk on coping, in which he stressed the three As — Accept (disability), Adjust (to the new situation) and Achieve (victory).

Accepting disability isn't always easy, but sometimes it is necessary to begin by accepting what cannot be changed. It doesn't mean giving up, but rather acknowledging the reality of a situation — that what has happened *has* indeed happened. In many cases, it is possible to find peace only with ourselves and others by accepting whatever has occurred.

To adjust means living in the present rather than in the past. The blinded chaplain had to find new ways of doing things, but he believed he *could* do it — and eventually he did just that.

Success doesn't usually come overnight, and demands grit and determination. However, when the person with a problem gets to the stage of being able to cope, he or she has certainly reached the achievement stage.

The minister in question, the late Rev. Geoffrey Treglown, ended his talk by sharing a helpful maxim from his mother: "Turn your face always to the sunshine, and the shadows will fall behind you."

Accept — Adjust — Achieve. It's not too difficult a challenge to remember, is it?

FRIDAY—JUNE 24.

EVELYN WOODLEY often sends me a thought with a message. In this one she reminds us all that we are not the victims of circumstances, that we *are* responsible for what we do and what we are:

> You had no part in choosing
> to live,
> but, you have the right
> to choose, *how* you live.

SATURDAY—JUNE 25.

THE 23rd Psalm with its message of peace, serenity and hope is a great favourite. I like this version from Japan by Toki Miyashina:

The Lord is my pace-setter, I shall not rush. He makes me stop for quiet intervals of rest; He provides me with images of stillness, which restore my serenity. He leads me in ways of efficiency through calmness of mind; and His guidance is peace. Even though I have a great many things to accomplish each day I will not fret; for His presence is here; His timelessness, His all-important will, keep me in balance. He prepares refreshment and renewal in the midst of my activity. By anointing my mind with the oils of tranquillity, my cup of joyous energy overflows. Surely harmony and effectiveness shall be the fruits of my hours; for I will walk in the peace of my Lord, and dwell in His house for ever.

SUNDAY—JUNE 26.

AND all the people came early in the morning to him in the temple, for to hear him.

Luke 21:38

TOGETHERNESS

THE FRIENDSHIP BOOK

HAVE you heard about Sheila Hocken and the chocolate-brown Labrador, Emma, her constant companion and guide dog? For many years Sheila was blind, depending on Emma to keep her out of danger and to be her "eyes".

Fortunately, a miracle operation restored Sheila's sight and the wonder of being able to see completely changed her life. It has made her happy to know that because she has told people what it is like to see for the very first time, they themselves look on everyday things with greater appreciation.

She recalls, in her book "Emma V.I.P.", a train journey from London: "As the train sped north to Nottingham, there was the most incredible sunset: great rays of red and gold through banks of slate-blue cloud as we reached the Trent . . .

"There were five others in the compartment with me, all businessmen. Three were asleep, one was doing a crossword and the other was hidden by his newspaper. I wanted to get on my seat and shout at them: 'Look! Wake up! Isn't it marvellous? Why don't you use your eyes for something important? Something wonderful that will never ever happen again exactly as it is now?' But I just sat there, and the eyes of those asleep remained closed, while the man doing the crossword gazed up momentarily, but sightlessly as he pondered a clue and the other man stayed hidden behind his paper . . ."

A SCHOOL examination paper asked the question, "Why do cocks crow early every morning?"

One 12-year-old replied: "My dad says they have to make the most of it while the hens are still asleep."

THE FRIENDSHIP BOOK

ONE morning I met my friend Bob taking his dog for a walk. It was some time since we had met for a chat, so I joined him for another lap around the park whilst we caught up with each other's news.

Bob told me he was feeling very pleased because he had just received a legacy from an elderly aunt, his inheritance as he called it. It was not a large amount, but sufficient to enable him to take his invalid wife on a much-needed holiday.

It's good when we receive a bonus of this sort which allows us to enjoy something which we might otherwise never have had. However, let's not forget all the good things that are constantly with us — our home and friends, the companionship of a loved pet, the solace of music and books and all that helps to make life pleasant. The list is endless.

So, let's take stock of our store of treasures and never minimise our own personal "inheritance".

ON the outside wall of a church in Edinburgh which thousands walk past each year, a group of Christian artists get together to paint topical and meaningful pictures. Local people and tourists often stop to admire and think about what they see.

The minister greatly values the work these dedicated artists are doing. "Many older people still visit churches regularly and see the message medieval artists left for us in the stained glass windows, but among the younger generation there are some who never see the inside of a church. These artists are taking the message outside to them."

In this way what would otherwise be a blank wall brings inspiration and beauty to many.

JULY

FRIDAY—JULY 1.

HOW I love to see the colourful displays of wallflower and forget-me-nots growing outside the walls and fences of many country gardens at this time of the year. The reason I like them so much (apart from their beauty, of course) is that they have been planted not for the benefit of the owners who aren't able to see them from inside the garden, but for the pleasure of all who pass by on foot, or on the road — city dwellers perhaps, on an outing.

It's one of those special acts of neighbourliness which do so much to cheer us all up.

Today, I raise my hat to all those who perform little, unsung acts of kindness — those who are ready to take on a bit of extra shopping when it is needed; those who take the thorns from a bunch of roses before presenting them; those who have the right word to say at the right time; those who plant flowers for the delight of others.

SATURDAY—JULY 2.

HAPPY CIRCLE

THERE are many folk around us
Lonely, sad — a little shy,
Those who sometimes feel forgotten
As the busy world goes by.
Let's expand our happy circle
Show the lonely that we care,
Draw them into friendship's keeping,
Friends are friendly, everywhere!

Elizabeth Gozney.

WHEN DAY IS DONE

THE FRIENDSHIP BOOK

F**OR** we are his workmanship, created in Christ Jesus unto good works, which God hath before ordained that we should walk in them.

Ephesians 2:10

I **HAVE** pinned this verse by Noel Scott above my desk where it will catch my eye every time I start to daydream!

Now it's all very well, just to sit down and dwell
On the jobs that you're planning to do,
For action is needed
To get those jobs speeded,
But who's going to do them? Are YOU?

L**AST** Summer, the Lady of the House and I found these lines about Time written on the clock in Chester Cathedral:

When as a child I laughed and wept —
Time crept
When as a youth I waxed more bold —
Time strolled
When I became a full grown man —
Time ran
When older still I grew
Time flew
Soon I shall find in passing on —
Time gone
O Christ will Thou have saved me then.
Amen.

H

THE FRIENDSHIP BOOK

AESOP told the story of a lion and a mouse. It was a hot day and the lion lay down to rest. The mouse came along, walked round the lion, and might have gone away unnoticed had she not tried to explore the beast's ear. At this the lion awoke in a rage and prepared to crush the mouse with his large paw, but the mouse begged for mercy and got her reprieve.

Twelve months later the lion became entangled in a net. Angrily he stamped about and roared, but the mesh tightened around him. When the mouse heard the lion she hurried to him and patiently gnawed at the rope until he was freed.

It's not unusual for the most underrated things to turn out to be of the most value, and few of us are so small or weak that we are unable to be of help in someone else's distress.

ONE summer I went with the Lady of the House to see an exhibition of embroidery at a London church. The tapestries were all worked by students from a school of needlework in the city.

I was very impressed by the work on show. The colours were blended exquisitely. An example of Swedish needle-weaving also caught my eye. A student was standing nearby and I asked her, "If a mistake is made, does the stitching have to be unpicked and re-done?"

"No," came the reply. "Our teacher is so artistic that when a mistake is made she can use a technique that makes the pattern look even more beautiful."

Later, as I pondered those words, I thought of the greater Teacher, who can take our mistakes and blend them into a pattern for the future far more meaningful than we could ever have imagined.

THE FRIENDSHIP BOOK

STEPPING STONES

*A*S we step one to another,
    O'er the swiftly flowing stream,
Every stone is like a brother —
    Something strong on which to lean.

Stepping stones provide a pathway,
    Where we can safely tread
Through the dangers of the currents,
    To the bank that lies ahead.

For these stones are prayers we offer,
    Sometimes prayers of others, too;
They're a foothold in life's problems,
    And they guide us safely through.

                    Margaret H. Dixon.

WHEN I switched on the television one evening, I heard a chef from a small holiday hotel saying, "I am not an eminent chef, nobody has heard of me, but I know that my work is always of the best, and I am proud of it."

This then made me think of a remark written by Sir Robin Day, the television journalist, in his book "Day By Day". He mentions the critics who called him arrogant and bad-tempered, and says that he had to learn not to get upset, because all good broadcasters must judge their own work by the exacting standards of skill and integrity, and this he always tried to do.

Many other men and women through the centuries have shown us that it is always wise to work conscientiously and with integrity. There is no greater achievement than doing our best.

THE FRIENDSHIP BOOK

GRACE be unto you, and peace, from God our Father, and from the Lord Jesus Christ.

Corinthians I 1:3

HAVE you heard the story about the little boy who was about to set off for Sunday School?

His mother gave him two coins, a 10p piece and a 20p piece, and said he could put whichever he wished in the collection plate. The other he could keep for himself.

When he came home again, his mother said, "Which coin did you put in the collection, Daniel?"

"Well," he replied, "I was going to put in the 20p, but just before the plate came round our teacher told us that the Lord loves a cheerful giver. When I thought about it I knew I should be more cheerful if I gave the 10p — so that's what I did!"

THE poet Barbara Jemison sent me these thoughtful lines:

> If I sat down and thought of all
> The things I haven't got,
> And numbered all the things I want,
> Gosh, there would be a lot!
>
> No doubt I'd either weep or moan,
> And my ill-luck deplore,
> Much better adding up my joys —
> And find them by the score.

THE FRIENDSHIP BOOK

THE Lady of the House and I called to see one of our old neighbours who had had to move into a small house without a garden because of poor health. We knew she would miss her lawns and flower borders but were surprised at the way she had already transformed her drab little back yard. She had filled tubs and containers with scarlet geraniums, colourful begonias and marigolds, and her hanging baskets were a cascade of fuchsias and trailing lobelia.

"I've chosen the brightest colours I could find," she said, "and what's more I have grown them all myself. In the Autumn I sat at my kitchen table and took cuttings and in the Spring I grew seeds on my sunny window sill — and now that the nice weather has arrived, all I have to do is go round with the watering can and sit in the sun enjoying the blooms."

As we walked home again the Lady of the House remarked, "What a lovely spirit Mrs Slater has! Whatever place becomes her home, she soon makes it into a bright and cheerful spot."

God bless all homemakers.

MY friend Andrew told me once that he had never forgotten a little verse which hung on his bedroom wall when he was a child:

You cannot set the whole world right,
Nor all the people in it.
You cannot do the work of years in just a
single minute.
But keep one little corner straight
By humble, patient labour,
And do the work that each hour brings —
And help your next-door neighbour.

FRIDAY—JULY 15.

SOMETIMES a well-meant word or gesture of encouragement at the right time is all that is needed to determine the course of somebody's life.

I am thinking of a story about Sir Walter Scott. When he was a boy, he contracted a fever which left him lame and very weak. As a result, it was thought that his life would not amount to much.

When he reached his teens, he was in the company of a number of famous writers, including Robert Burns. Underneath a picture on the wall was a line or two of verse which attracted Burns' attention. He asked who wrote it, but nobody seemed to know. Timidly, young Walter plucked up courage to give the name, quoting the rest of the little-known writer's poem.

Burns was very impressed. Laying his hand on the boy's head he said, "Ah, my boy, I'm sure you'll be a great man some day."

Perhaps that word of encouragement spurred on the lad for he became Scotland's great novelist and poet. He is remembered particularly for his Waverley Novels and, of course, his imposing 200-foot memorial in East Princes Street Gardens is seen by thousands every year. A great man indeed.

SATURDAY—JULY 16.

I CAN'T vouch for the truth of it, but I heard of a church where there were two notices on the board, side by side.

The first invited attendance at a special meeting to listen to a guest speaker on the subject of "HELL — do you know what it is?", while the second simply said, "Come along on Sunday to listen to our new organist."

THE FRIENDSHIP BOOK

THE heavens declare the glory of God; and the firmament sheweth his handywork.

Psalms 19:1

MANY worthy people live by the precept, "It is more blessed to give than to receive". In fact, they find it hard to accept anything by way of thanks, quite forgetting that maybe the other person needs a blessing as well!

Last year, a tree blew down in a neighbour's garden, and he decided to cut it up for logs. He found he had a great pile of them, probably more than he'd need for the coming Winter, so he filled a sack and took it along to a pensioner who lives nearby. She was delighted, as she loves the crackle of a blazing log fire.

"Now," she said to her neighbour, "lots of my cooking apples came down in that same gale, so you must take a bag home."

"Oh, no, thanks," he replied awkwardly, and was stunned when she said drily, "Your back'll ache shouldering those logs home again!" Fortunately, they both have a sense of humour and he took her point — and the apples.

THE young lad who lives nearby was on his way home from school when he stopped to ask me, "Mr Gay, what did the first magnet say to the second magnet?"

"I've no idea," I replied.

" 'You're very attractive.' "

Next time I must have a riddle of my own ready.

THE FRIENDSHIP BOOK

IN QUIETNESS

GO deeper into silence;
Put aside the worldly din;
Go past the ticking of the clock,
And hear the voice within.

Go deeper into silence;
Still your body, mind and soul,
And listen to the voice of God:
The voice that makes you whole.

Marion Elliott.

THERE are two sides to every story and this was brought home to me when a gardener friend happened to mention that he likes to see a few plants with greyish leaves in his garden because they are great harmonisers. When I thought about it, I could see what he meant, for too much brilliance can be overpowering and it is good to have a few restful grey patches in between, whether they be in our garden or in life in general.

So today, I think with gratitude of all those who help us to see things from a new angle and to widen our scope of appreciation.

WHY do the compilers of word-puzzles frequently say, "No two-letter words permitted"? Two-letter words can be just as important as longer ones. Just consider this cryptic and candid sentence: "If it is to be, it is up to me."

SATURDAY—JULY 23.

AS I was walking down the street, I glanced at a notice in the window of one of the small shops that sell sandwiches, salads, cakes and other snacks. It said "Fresh Supplies Daily".

I began to look at the people passing by — some looked tired, others down and anxious. Then I began to look for somebody who looked cheerful and at peace. I did not see many. The pace of modern life makes considerable demands on us all these days, and we are often living in a state of tension.

We certainly all need "Fresh Supplies Daily" and the answer is to be found only within ourselves. Loving and caring for others and being considerate in the course of our everyday lives can create a contented mind — a necessity for a happy day, not only for us, but for others, too.

SUNDAY—JULY 24.

FOR ye know the grace of our Lord Jesus Christ, that, though he was rich, yet for your sakes he became poor, that ye through his poverty might be rich.

Corinthians II 8:9

MONDAY—JULY 25.

WE don't choose the names we're given by our parents, but it's entirely up to us to create the reputations attached to them. Just think, our names mean the promises we keep in life — loyalty, faithfulness, honesty and truth.

In fact, our name is the blueprint of our character. "What's in a name?" asks Shakespeare's Juliet.

My answer is — everything we do.

TUESDAY—JULY 26.

LOVE, in one sense or another, plays an all-important part in our lives. I collect sayings and thoughts on the subject and recently I added this Eastern gem:

"Love is a fragile thing; it is like a glass which shatters if you hold it too tightly or too loosely."

WEDNESDAY—JULY 27.

WE are all inclined to think we could handle things better than those in charge of great events. How many of us, though, are truly capable of making the many vital decisions called for from those in positions of responsibility and authority?

It's an awesome thought to have such power over others, and thinking about this reminds me of the story of the considerate farmer — he wanted to show appreciation for his farmhand's heavy manual work by giving him a light job for the day, so he asked him to sort and size potatoes.

At lunch-time he went outside to speak to him, but found his employee looking very worried and agitated.

"What's the trouble?" asked the farmer.

"I don't mind work, sir," exclaimed the man, "but it's those awful decisions I have to make now!"

THURSDAY—JULY 28.

MANY eminent ministers and theologians have written thoughtful words about prayer, but I always like this short sentence written by George Herbert many years ago:

"Prayer should be the key of the day and the lock of the night."

PRECIOUS MOMENTS

FRIDAY—JULY 29.

WE were travelling with friends on the A1 road, hoping to spend an afternoon and evening discovering York on the way to a conference elsewhere. It was outside Stamford that it happened — our car just stopped! It had to be towed to a garage, and we were told that it would not be ready until the next day. It was very disappointing.

Our friends stayed the night at a motel, while the Lady of the House and I decided to discover Stamford. What a beautiful little place it is with its attractive stone Georgian buildings! It was a lovely discovery, so that in one way we were pleased about the breakdown.

Have you ever noticed that life can be like this little adventure? If we have the right positive attitude, then disappointments can often be turned into blessings.

SATURDAY—JULY 30.

I PUT on my clothes,
With neatness and pride,
Put on my make-up,
Spots and wrinkles to hide.
Brush up my hair,
Think it's all been worthwhile,
Gosh — I nearly forgot,
I must put on my smile!

Phyllis Ellison.

SUNDAY—JULY 31.

SEEK ye the Lord while he may be found, call ye upon him while he is near.

Isaiah 55:6

AUGUST

MONDAY—AUGUST 1.

"**I** HAVE an old scrapbook inherited from a favourite aunt," writes Barbara Jemison. "In it she jotted down verses that appealed to her. Here is one of them I specially like."

I like it, too:

Now here's to you, and here's to yours,
 Good health — good luck — good cheer!
Unbroken may the circle be
 This day and time next year.
If fortune smiles on you and yours,
 Thank God for troubles gone;
And if the way be hard, may God
 Give strength to battle on.

TUESDAY—AUGUST 2.

ONE of the gardens featured on the television programme "Gardeners' World" was that of Colin Cashmore of Midway in South Derbyshire. Anne Swithinbank, one of the presenters, referred to it as the most colourful back garden she had ever seen, and indeed it was a riot of brightly-coloured beds, borders and hanging baskets.

Mr Cashmore had spent his working life underground as a miner and when he came to retirement, he wondered how he would occupy his days — growing vegetables perhaps, keeping whippets, racing, or cultivating flowers — the flowers won. Now his beautiful garden is an ever-open door for visitors and, as he says, "My pleasure is in giving other people pleasure."

THE FRIENDSHIP BOOK

WHAT a strange place the countryside must seem to a child who has always lived in an urban area. I liked a story in this context told by the birdman Tony Soper.

One day, a schoolmaster had taken a class from a city school to study Nature in the country. As they investigated the rich variety of flowers and insects, one little lad wandered off and startled a skylark from its nest. He looked in amazement as the bird soared upwards and hovered above, singing merrily. After watching a minute or so, as the bird remained poised in the air, he ran back to his teacher and called, "Come and look at this sparrer. It can't get up and can't get down and it ain't 'arf 'ollering!"

The ways of Nature are indeed wonderful, especially in the eyes of a nine-year-old Cockney!

ONE day, Peggy, busy with her weekly washing, glanced through the kitchen window just as her neighbour was pegging a pair of pyjamas on the clothes-line. In the seat of the trousers was a huge tear.

Peggy smiled to herself, knowing exactly what she was going to do. She waited until the coast was clear, went round to Dorothy's garden, took the pyjamas off the line, and came home.

Fifteen minutes later, the tear neatly patched with the help of her sewing-machine, Peggy replaced the pyjamas on the line.

She happened to know that Dorothy didn't have a sewing-machine and was a poor needlewoman. Lending her neighbour a helping hand made Peggy's day worthwhile, and it gave Dorothy a lovely surprise, too.

FRIDAY—AUGUST 5.

THERE'S nothing the Lady of the House and I enjoy more than to wrap up warmly and go for a brisk evening walk when "the winds are breathing low, and the stars are shining bright." It blows all the cobwebs away and certainly helps us to sleep more soundly!

William Hazlitt enjoyed his walks, too. He wrote: "I can enjoy society in a room, but out of doors, Nature is company enough for me."

The philosopher Kierkegaard gave this advice to his niece who was inclined to be a hypochondriac: "Above all, do not lose your desire to walk. Every day I walk myself into a state of well-being and walk away from every illness. I have walked myself into my best thoughts, and I know of no thought so burdensome that one cannot walk away from it."

So here's to that pleasant pastime of walking and the many benefits it brings us!

SATURDAY—AUGUST 6.

I LIKE the story about the teacher who was asked if he taught his pupils religion.

"I teach it all day long," he replied. "I teach it in arithmetic by accuracy, in history by humanity and in astronomy by reverence. And I teach it by kindness to animals, good manners to others and by truthfulness in all things."

Truly, religion has a place in everything we do!

SUNDAY—AUGUST 7.

NOW unto God and our Father be glory for ever and ever. Amen.

Philippians 4:20

H

THE FRIENDSHIP BOOK

OUR friends Alice and Bob are pensioners. The Lady of the House went to see them the other afternoon.

"Come in," said Alice. "Go straight through to the kitchen." Bob was sitting there, patiently packing a box with biscuits, tins and jars. It seems that their granddaughter Judith is at a city university, and a friend of theirs was going to be passing through and had promised to take the parcel for them. Judith had just moved from the halls of residence to a flat with friends. Alice and Bob felt sure that she would welcome a few little luxuries and as they had just cashed their pensions they had gone out and bought all sorts of things, which they now eagerly showed us.

As the Lady of the House and I talked about it afterwards, we wondered who would get the most pleasure from the parcel — the grandparents or Judith?

HAVE you ever wondered what to do — or what to do next?

Some unknown poet has produced a little verse which reminds us that if something needs to be done, now is the time to do it:

What time is it?
Time to do well,
Time to live better,
Give up that grudge,
Answer that letter,
Speak the kind word to sweeten a sorrow,
Do that kind deed you would leave till tomorrow.

Tomorrow is likely to be so much sweeter as a result — for yourself and for others!

THE FRIENDSHIP BOOK

I RECENTLY said another "thank you" to a man who has given me musical pleasure and satisfaction for many, many years. No, he's not one of the famous composers or musicians of our time, but a railwayman who spent all his life in the Rhondda Valley — John Hughes.

It was John Hughes who, in the mid-20th century, took the words of the hymn "Guide me, O Thou Great Jehovah, pilgrim through this barren land" and set them to a tune which must have been spiritually inspired, one he called Cwm Rhondda after his home town.

The words of this wonderful hymn were written by an 18th-century clergyman and hymn writer, William Williams. He was a popular hymn-writer of that time, but the words of "Guide me, O Thou Great Jehovah" with its strong call to the Great Creator to guide man through life, to strengthen, sustain and shield him against all ills, and then to lead him safely into the Promised Land, were given new life by the glorious soaring cadences of John Hughes' tune. Just to sing Cwm Rhondda is an inspiration, so obviously John Hughes was inspired, too.

Come to think of it, there are so many people we should say thank you to — and it is much better to say these words now while they are still alive.

I TURNED up a very good bit of advice the other day from Apostolius, who in the 15th century had become a refugee from Constantinople.

He advised: "While you are making new friends, don't forget the old ones."

A timely reminder, don't you think?

THE FRIENDSHIP BOOK

I N this simple verse, Phyllis Ellison tells us some of the things to look forward to when our working days are over:

You can rise when you want,
Do as you please,
Work in the garden,
Or just sit at ease.
Your options are many,
Every day will inspire,
For a new life begins
On the day you retire.

W E once travelled to Austria for a holiday, and after arriving home I wondered if the Lady of the House had really enjoyed herself. I immediately put on the kettle while she relaxed in a comfortable armchair.

"Well, Francis, going abroad for a holiday helps us to appreciate all the everyday things that we take for granted. I suppose it's because they are always there, that we don't notice them until they're not around."

"Yes," I replied, enjoying my cup of tea. "It's the same with people. We often don't even notice them until they aren't there. We tend to take them all for granted; our family, friends and neighbours, the milkman and the postman. We should speak to them all and say 'thank you' more often."

T HE man departed, and told the Jews that it was Jesus, which had made him whole.

John 5:15

TWO WORLDS

THE FRIENDSHIP BOOK

RUTH GRAHAM, wife of the evangelist Billy Graham, once told a story about a respected elderly black man who had worked for a certain family for many years and was a trusted friend. When one of the family was about to be married, old Abe called on him.

"I want to give you a bit of advice," he said. "When I go out into the fields to plant corn and my wife Mandy goes along with me, I tell her what I want her to do. And she minds me, 'cause that's *my* territory.

"Now, after I've finished the day's work and walk into the kitchen with my muddy shoes and Mandy says, 'Now, Abe, you get your dirty feet out of my kitchen floor!' I mind her — 'cause that's *her* territory."

Well, it seems a very good principle to establish parameters in marriage as in any other relationship — as long as we are prepared to reverse roles as soon as illness or any other problem makes it necessary.

JIM and I often travel on the same bus so we know each other quite well and enjoy a chat as we wait in the queue.

Recently he had a small operation and he was telling me all about it. "I realised how afraid I was of the anaesthetic," he said, "and with four small children everything seemed a big risk, especially entrusting my life to people I didn't know while I was helpless — it was a dreadful thought."

"I know just how you felt," I said. Then Jim went on, "Of course, all went well, and there was no need to be afraid, but I now realise that a brave person is not one who has no fear, but one who overcomes it!"

Wise words indeed.

THE FRIENDSHIP BOOK

WEDNESDAY—AUGUST 17.

YOU cannot help noticing how we are living in times of great change. Sometimes it can all be so confusing that we may wonder if anything will remain constant.

I liked the little story told by Lloyd Douglas, author of "The Robe". One morning he met a violin-maker. "Good morning," the violin-maker said.

"What's good about it?" asked the author.

"Oh, this," said the violin-maker as he picked up his tuning fork and sounded 'A'. He struck it and said, " 'A' is 'A' today and it was so yesterday. 'A' will be 'A' 1000 years from now."

So if you should fear anything in this quickly changing world, remember the violin-maker's 'A'. Remember, too, the three great virtues — Faith, Hope and Love — which will always be constant, yesterday, today, and tomorrow.

THURSDAY—AUGUST 18.

IT seems a long time ago now, but I can still see the scene and remember the conversation as if it were yesterday.

We lived in another small village at the time, and always attended the little church on Sunday evenings. One Summer we were walking home with 80-year-old Wilfred, a smallholder all his working life. We were discussing the sermon which had been on the subject of how there is always some good to be found in the worst of us if others would only look for it.

"Would you say that's true, Wilfred?" asked the Lady of the House. He thought for a minute or two, and then answered, "Aye! Every day God makes silk purses out of sows' ears."

A sermon in a few words that I'll never forget.

PARADISE FOUND

THE FRIENDSHIP BOOK

WHEN the Lady of the House celebrates her birthday, the cards and gifts she receives from friends and relatives express lovely messages of friendship.

Reflecting on "gifts" and the motivation behind them, I was reminded of some delightful lines written by Arthur Balfour:

The best thing to give your enemy is forgiveness;
To an opponent, tolerance;
To a friend, your heart;
To a child, a good example;
To a father, deference;
To a mother, conduct that will make her proud of you;
To yourself, respect;
To all men, charity.

A FEW years ago I was invited to look in on a young friend's birthday party. There, I met five-year-old Kerry who recounted in graphic detail the story of Noah's Ark. Kerry ended by saying, "And then God made this great, fantastic rainbow to remind everyone he was their friend."

Now I can hardly wait to see my next rainbow. A reminder like that I don't mind!

BLESSED are they that do his commandments, that they may have right to the tree of life, and may enter in through the gates into the city.

Revelation 22:14

WHEN your vision seems quite cloudy
  And you cannot see the way,
Don't be too ambitious,
  Just think about today.
You'll find, as God has promised
  That you have your daily bread,
Thank Him for this moment,
  Then you'll see the way ahead.

Jean Harris.

WE are fortunate to have a small shop in our village. The owner knows all his customers well — their faults, their strengths, and, above all, their circumstances. Many a time I have seen him add a bit extra, letting the scales pull down a little more weightily, for a customer who is having a bad time financially.

Once when someone was buying an extra batch of groceries and happened to mention that they were for old Mrs James who wasn't too well, he popped in a bar of chocolate, saying, "Tell her they're from an admirer — she's a grand old lady. She's not had it easy, you know."

A customer standing next to me muttered, "That man'll go bankrupt one day."

Oh, no, not him — I'm sure of that. He may not gather great monetary wealth or worldly goods, but in things of the spirit Tom will always have a never-ending store of riches. He'll not have cause to look back on his life with a guilty conscience, or an uneasy feeling that he "could have done better." In the account that really matters, he's well in credit.

THE FRIENDSHIP BOOK

IT came as a surprise to hear that there is a tape titled "Sound Of Silence". That is exactly what it is — an hour of silence.

It was the idea of members of the historic Unitarian Chapel in Lewes, Sussex, as part of their fundraising effort for major restoration work on the 400-year-old building. Admittedly, the tape commences with traffic sounds, but then it continues in complete silence.

It made me realise that silence is a commodity we rather take for granted as we do those other precious gifts such as the sun, the rain, the wind and the fresh air. It is to be found in a quiet corner of a park, on a hill top, within the pages of a good book, and in a country churchyard — and in countless places known only to ourselves.

Today, let's remember those lovely words of Gerard Manley Hopkins:

> *Elected Silence, sing to me*
> *And beat upon my whorlèd ear,*
> *Pipe me to pastures still and be*
> *The music that I care to hear.*

> *A SMILE can be a ray of sun*
> *To brighten up the dark.*
> *A smile can show a sense of fun*
> *Has made its merry mark.*
> *A smile can be the guiding light,*
> *That hope can often bring.*
> *A smile can be a happy sight;*
> *Try it — that's the thing!*

J. M. Robertson.

BRIGHT HAVEN

HAVE you ever thought how our actions today can affect circumstances in the years ahead? Here is a story which illustrates an example of this:

A gentleman was building a country house, and had reached the stage when he was planning the garden. He had an elderly gardener to help him, so he gave him instructions on where he wanted the apple and walnut trees planted.

The old man listened to the owner's suggestions, but did not follow them.

"I have planted the walnut trees where you told me to put the apple trees, and vice versa," he told him afterwards, "because when they're grown, the walnuts will shade the apple trees."

From his wealth of experience he foresaw how the garden would be in years to come.

It is wise to look to the future and consider, not just how things will affect us in our own lifetime, but how they will affect others in generations to come.

SATURDAY—AUGUST 27.

THE actor Alec McCowen gave very many performances of his successful dramatic reading of St Mark's Gospel.

On one occasion he gave a performance to a large number of bishops and other clergy. "It was," he remarked afterwards, "the first time in history that an actor had 400 prompters!"

SUNDAY—AUGUST 28.

TO God only wise, be glory through Jesus Christ for ever. Amen.

Romans 16:27

THE FRIENDSHIP BOOK

DON'T keep it quiet, but share it,
And pass it round about —
Good news is always welcome
So say it — with a shout!

Anne Kreer.

HAVE you found that when you have a problem worrying you, it helps if you undertake a task that is physically tiring? Our friend May was in that position recently. She had been unwell and was waiting to see a specialist at the hospital.

One evening when she was alone and her thoughts kept coming back to her health, she decided to tackle a long-overdue household job. She has some silver plate which had become very tarnished, so she set to and cleaned it until it was positively gleaming.

As she replaced the clean silver on her shelves, she realised that she hadn't had time to think about herself all the time she had been working.

I am pleased to tell you that, when she saw the specialist, he gave her a clean bill of health. As May says, her worries were needless, but she learned a valuable lesson, and one she won't forget.

IN the great tapestry of life
What colour do I weave?
A golden thread of happiness
Is what I'd like to leave.
But maybe I'm a crimson
or a purple or a white,
Well, life needs every colour
To keep the pattern bright.

# SEPTEMBER

THURSDAY—SEPTEMBER 1.

*T*READING *along the road of life,*
  Battling day by day,
People omit an important thing
  If they forget to pray.
Tempted to think you can't keep on?
  Lift up your head and say,
What I can't do, God will do for me,
  Once I begin to pray.

Barbara Jemison.

FRIDAY—SEPTEMBER 2.

IT'S September and we are entering the ninth month of the year, although for the Romans it was the seventh month. The Anglo-Saxons called it "Gerst-monath", Barley Month, and that describes it beautifully.

It is the golden month, one of warm, still, and mellow days. Corn has been gathered in, apples are ready for harvesting, flowers in herbaceous borders are quietly preparing for Autumn, and we can anticipate a rest from many of our outdoor tasks.

I can happily echo the words of Alex Smith about September:

Best I love September's yellow,
Morns of dew-strung gossamer,
Thoughtful days without a stir;
Rooky clamours, brazen leaves,
Stubble dotted o'er with sheaves —
More than Spring's bright uncontrol
Suit the Autumn of my soul.

THE FRIENDSHIP BOOK

WHEN I went to the kitchen drawer to look for a piece of string, I saw that it was full of green tomatoes. I wasn't surprised to find them there, for I had not long since brought them in from the greenhouse — the last of the season's crop — and I guessed that the Lady of the House had put them there to ripen.

"But surely this doesn't belong?" I protested, picking out a large, bright red tomato.

"Oh, yes, Francis," said the Lady of the House. "I have put that there to help the others to turn. It's an encourager. They will ripen much more quickly with the red one amongst them."

So, thoughtfully I replaced the red tomato. There is a lesson for life in this, I believe. At some time or other most of us encounter trouble in our lives. We all know how much a friendly word can mean to us when we are feeling down, and it's not hard to imagine that our encouragement might be just what someone else needs.

BE thou exalted, O God, above the heavens: let thy glory be above all the earth.

Psalms 57:11

IN an American magazine which friends gave me, I came across this little maxim which made me stop and think:

I bumped my head again while getting into the car. Come to think of it — most of the bumps in life come when we forget to lower our head.

K

THE FRIENDSHIP BOOK

TODAY I will spend some time with a needle attempting to get bramble thorns out of my sore fingers. A yearly ritual this, since I was a boy, but one that I wouldn't miss. Each Autumn I go, stick in hand, bucket swinging, out to the country and reap Nature's "free fruit".

This annual jaunt means more than just a prospect of delicious tarts and jams. To me, it means re-uniting in an activity that I have shared with others all my life.

I thank God every September for the wild fruit and the loving companionship that goes with collecting it.

A BISHOP'S crook — reminding us that he is a good shepherd — seems to me to add a final touch of dignity and authority to that office. A story is told of Bishop Harvey Goodwin of Carlisle, who was leaving the home of one of his rectors after a visit. The rector's daughter was watching, quite fascinated, as the good man packed away his crook in a convenient carrying case. To please her the bishop reassembled it in all its glory.

"What is it for?" she asked.

"It's very useful. The pointed end is to urge on clergy who don't go fast enough, while the crook is to hold back those who go too fast!" came the reply.

A very different story tells of a pupil writing home from boarding school. He wrote:

"The Bishop came for confirmation, and from my seat in the choir I had a good view of him. Now I know what a crook looks like!"

I'm sure the young lad's parents knew exactly what he meant.

THE FRIENDSHIP BOOK

A READER in an old folks' home sent me the following, which, she says, is pinned up on the wall of the day lounge:

"We were born before television, before penicillin, before polio shots, frozen foods, Xerox, plastic, and contact lenses. We were before credit cards, laser beams, ballpoint pens; before dishwashers, electric blankets, tumble dryers — and before man walked on the moon.

"We were before day-care centres, group therapy, and nursing homes. We had never heard of FM radio, tape decks, electric typewriters, artificial hearts, word processors, yoghurt — and men wearing earrings. For us, a 'chip' meant something that went with fish, hardware meant hardware, and software wasn't even a word!

"No wonder we are sometimes confused, and that there is often a generation gap. The main thing is we have survived. Let's celebrate that fact every day!"

THANK YOU

WE thank you for the many things
That you have blessed today —
The flowers and trees,
The birds and bees,
The children at their play.

Dear Lord, we ask so many things
To heal, forgive and bless.
So thank you, too,
For all you do
To give us happiness.

Dorothy M. Loughran.

AGAINST THE GRAIN

THE FRIENDSHIP BOOK

PERHAPS you have heard the story of the two mice that fell into a tub of cream?

The first one looked at the straight slippery sides, lost heart, decided there was no possible way he could get out, and drowned. The second one, however, thought that there must be a way to save himself so he started swimming while he considered the problem. Eventually, as he paddled around, the cream turned into butter and so he was able to climb out of the tub.

The moral? It is not always the situation we find ourselves in that leads to our downfall — but the way we tackle that situation.

Steve Davis, the well-known snooker champion, once said, "It may not be your fault for being down, but it's got to be your fault for not getting up."

BUT Jesus called them unto him, and said, Suffer little children to come unto me, and forbid them not: for of such is the kingdom of God.

Luke 18:16

I LIKE this Hebrew prayer which I read recently. Perhaps you would like to make it your own prayer today:

Give me the strength to meet each day
With quiet will,
Give me the faith to know Thou art
My Shepherd still.
Give me the light to find my way
When shadows fall,
Be Thou my steady guiding star,
Father of all.

THE FRIENDSHIP BOOK

AT the beginning of Creation, it is said, none of the plants had any colour but green until God sent an angel to give each flower its own special hue — yellow for the daffodils, white for the daisies, red for the poppies and so on. Only one was forgotten, a climbing shrub growing in a corner. It felt sad to think it had been overlooked, but it carried on growing to the best of its ability in its own little spot.

In the Autumn the angel came again to check on how the plants were doing. When the creeper was seen to be growing in spite of its disappointment, it was commended for its faithfulness. The plant was quite overcome by the praise and a fiery blush spread over it. Now the Virginia Creeper is grown as an ornamental shrub on the walls of many houses, and each Autumn its bright green leaves turn to a glorious shade of red as it remembers the angel's praise.

"IT'S impossible — I can't do it!" We have all said that at some time or another. Next time you are tempted to do so, remember the pendulum . . . that it was waiting to be fixed in place, and it began to calculate for how long it would be expected to tick — day and night — 60 seconds in a minute, 60 seconds in the hour, 24 hours in a day, and 365 days in a year. That amounted to millions of ticks! It would never be able to manage it, decided the pendulum.

"Do just one tick at a time," the clockmaker advised. "That's all that's expected of you."

So the pendulum began, just one tick at a time, and it is still ticking to this day. As the Chinese proverb says, a journey of a thousand miles must begin with a single step.

THE FRIENDSHIP BOOK

I CAME across this humorous story in a church magazine, and would like to share it with you today. A visitor to a classroom of seven-year-olds noticed a sad, weary expression on the face of a little girl apparently trying to write a poem, so he stopped to look at her work.

Yesterday, yesterday, yesterday
Happiness, happiness, happiness
Today, today, today
Trouble, trouble, trouble
Tomorrow, tomorrow, tomorrow
Sorrow, sorrow, sorrow.

Very moved by these thoughts, he asked what had inspired her to write like this. She looked blank for a moment, then explained that it wasn't a poem. These words were her spelling mistakes being corrected!

I OFTEN listen to the news bulletins on the radio. It is, on occasion, a case of all doom and gloom, so I prefer not to pay too much attention. Besides, the complicated doings of politicians and international affairs can seem to have little relevance to the daily lives of ordinary folk.

Every now and then however, a little item with a difference will catch my ear. For instance, one day I heard that a lady had gained her pilot's licence at the age of 78. It was something she had always wanted to do, so she took a course of flying lessons and passed, to prove to herself and others that she could do it.

The radio commentator said what a remarkable example to us all she was. At whatever age we find ourselves, there is always something to be achieved.

THE FRIENDSHIP BOOK

LOOKING AHEAD

"*IF only", and "it might have been"*
Are bitter words to feel,
   You cannot turn the clock way back,
    As though it were a wheel.
It's wiser to forget the past,
   Regrets are hard to bear,
The present and the future
   Offer finer things to share.
What e'er it was you left undone,
   Or did not mean to do,
Just turn the pages of the book,
   And start again anew.
Each morning brings another chance
   To try in every way,
To look ahead with faith and hope,
   Towards a brighter day.

                Elizabeth Gozney.

THEREFORE whosoever heareth these sayings of mine, and doeth them, I will liken him unto a wise man, which built his house upon a rock.

                Matthew 7:24

THERE is an old saying: "If there is sufficient mud thrown around, some sticks." Unfortunately, it is only too true, and that's why we have to watch that "unruly member", the tongue, when we're chatting to a friend. Now, wouldn't it be wonderful if we could reverse that old saying and word it, thus:

"If there is sufficient sunshine flashed around, some penetrates."

RAINBOW ROAD

THE FRIENDSHIP BOOK

THE following very moving verses are said to have been found by the bedside of a dead Canadian airman:

Almighty and All-present power,
Short is the prayer I make to Thee,
I do not ask in battle hour
Any shield to cover me.

The vast inalienable way,
From which the stars do not depart
May not be turned aside to stay
The bullet flying to my heart.

I ask no help to strike my foe,
I seek no petty victory here,
The enemy I hate, I know
To Thee is dear.

But this I pray, be by my side
When death is drawing through the sky.
Almighty Lord, who also died
Teach me the way that I should die.

HAVE you heard the story about the Carmelite monk who was comparing his Order with others?

"For scholarship, of course," he said, "we can't compare with the Benedictines; and for good works we can't compare with the Franciscans; but, when it comes to humility, we're better than either of them."

Perhaps not what he really meant to convey!

THE FRIENDSHIP BOOK

IN this busy and stressful world of today some people are turning for help to relaxation exercises. Some jog, some try Yoga and breathing exercises, while others resort to mind relaxation courses. I have tried some of these, too — but they just don't work for me!

Let me tell you what does help me: It is just being at home.

When I am restless or in distress, I close our door on the world and find peace and quiet in simple joys: our kitten on the rug beside the fire; the kettle singing, and a home-made cake with a cup of tea from a familiar cup; my old slippers and all the things I have grown to love — a lamp, a vase, a clock.

The outside world of disillusionment has gone. I am happy and relaxed again. It is amongst our homely things that I am at peace.

HAVE you ever made a special rainbow? Poets and musicians have often written about them, and when I passed our small school playground recently, some children were busily arranging mirrors beside a shallow tray of water. I asked what they were doing and was told that they were "making a rainbow"!

I smiled to myself because I like to make rainbows, too, but not with mirrors. I secretly try to find something lovely every day, and I call it "My Rainbow".

From now on, I think that my special rainbow will be the sight of those four children with happy faces in the Spring sunshine trying to make *their* rainbow.

If we look for beauty always and everywhere, we can find it in the most unlikely places.

THE FRIENDSHIP BOOK

MY dictionary defines a friend as a person well known to another and regarded with liking, affection and loyalty — in fact, someone on our side and not hostile to our interests.

I once read that if you want a man to be a friend, ask him to do you a favour, while Dumas described friendship as "Forgetting what one gives and remembering what one receives."

Here's another thought on the subject: "If you want one year's prosperity, grow grain. If you want ten years' prosperity, grow men and women."

Most of all, though, I like what Robert Louis Stevenson wrote: "A friend is a present you give yourself."

I'm all in favour of a present like that!

CHARITY suffereth long, and is kind; charity envieth not; charity vaunteth not itself, is not puffed up.

Corinthians I 13:4

WHEN Noah first built the Ark, so it is said, it sprung a leak and emergency repairs had to be carried out.

First of all, the dog was sent for to plug the hole with his nose, but the water still came through. Next, Noah's wife was asked to put her hand there, but it still wasn't sufficient to stop the flow. Finally, Noah came and sat in the hole.

That is why, they say, a dog still has a cold nose, a lady has cold hands, and a gentleman likes to stand with his back to the fire!

THE FRIENDSHIP BOOK

WE have an old chest in the attic in which we keep a family Bible, Great-grandma's wedding dress — and some diaries. Now and again we browse through these. The other evening we were looking at journals kept by Great-aunt Maud and Uncle Percy.

"Have you noticed, Francis," said the Lady of the House, "that Maud kept her diary right to the last day of her life, and she always found something of interest to report, while Percy often wrote, 'Nothing much happened today'?"

It made us both think. Things are *always* going on around us that we can be pleased and happy about. Maud noticed them, but perhaps Percy never took the trouble to look.

I don't need to tell you which of them had the more fulfilling life. Maud is remembered for the kindly interest she took in family and friends while Percy is rarely mentioned, because no one knew him really well.

OUR friend Hazel had an accident while visiting London one day, and ended up in hospital with all sorts of unexpected complications.

Sometimes she felt very weak, and wondered what the future might hold, but then she uttered a little prayer which I commend to you. It is also known as an "old preacher's greeting":

"Lord, help me to remember that nothing is going to happen to me today that You and I can't handle together."

I am happy to report that Hazel is now back home and coping well.

THE FRIENDSHIP BOOK

WEATHER REPORT

WHEN you stop to think about it,
It's a fact that can amaze —
Your face is like the weather
In so many little ways . . .

You can be a ray of sunshine
With an ever-present smile.
A look that's cold and frosty
Can put Winter on your dial.

A deep depression's imminent
With traces of a frown.
A grin that spreads from East to West,
By thunder, earns renown.

Your face is like the weather,
And it's often up to you
To demonstrate your preference
For skies of grey — or blue.

J.M. Robertson.

THERE is an old-fashioned red telephone box inside a cathedral! It can be found at Liverpool's Anglican cathedral. Sir Gilbert Scott, the cathedral's architect, also designed the traditional-style telephone box so British Telecom presented one to the building. Something of grandeur and something of great everyday use both sprang from the mind of this inventive man.

It occurred to me as I read about this, that there is another difference between a telephone box and a cathedral — in a telephone box we speak to each other while in a cathedral we speak to God.

# OCTOBER

SATURDAY—OCTOBER 1.

DID you know the little rhyme which goes with the Big Ben chimes that precede the striking of the hours?

Lord, through this hour
Be Thou our guide
That by Thy power
No foot shall slide.

No wonder so many find inspiration in those loved and reassuring sounds.

We cannot stop time passing, but we can choose to use it wisely — with a little help.

SUNDAY—OCTOBER 2.

AND this is the will of him that sent me, that every one which seeth the Son, and believeth on him, may have everlasting life: and I will raise him up at the last day.

John 6:40

MONDAY—OCTOBER 3.

*A*UTUMN *leaves come fluttering past*
In bronze and gold array,
Soon Winter's rain and stormy blast
Will carry them away.

It's best to banish hopeless dreams
Which fade, like Autumn's leaves,
And start afresh on happier themes
That steadfastness achieves.

Dorothy M. Loughran.

AUTUMN WOODS

THE FRIENDSHIP BOOK

WHEN a visiting preacher gave his sermon one Sunday, he noticed a young boy busily scribbling in a notebook. The theme of the sermon was "What is God like?" and the preacher had been firm in telling his congregation that they should not think of God as an old man with a long, white beard sitting up in the sky.

After the service the preacher noticed the boy's notebook lying on one of the pews and he couldn't resist having a quick look. Inside he found a caricature of himself in the pulpit, and looking down on him from a cloud was an old man with a white beard saying, "Well, how does *he* know?"

The preacher thought that he had given a sermon, but he had been given one himself instead.

EACH October the Lady of the House buys pink hyacinths and has fun planting them in bowls to give to friends. They are not the bulbs specially prepared to flower at Christmas, but the ordinary ones which flower much later on in January or February.

"You see, Francis," she said, "there's so much going on at Christmas that people haven't time to notice the gradual daily growth of the hyacinths, but in the bleak January days, when all outside is sleeping, you can really appreciate their glossy leaves. Then as the flower begins to show, you know it won't be long before the room is filled with gorgeous perfume. I think it's the waiting for them to bloom that's the best part of it," she added.

I'm sure she is right. Like so many other things in life, the anticipation is often at least as sweet as the realisation, for the full pleasure is yet to come.

THE FRIENDSHIP BOOK

GIVE a little kindness,
Give it every day,
Give a little tenderness
As you go on your way.
The well of Love is endless,
And as long as you may live,
You'll find the more you give your love,
The more there'll be to give.

HAVE we become too lazy in our speech and the way we greet others?

An editor of an American fashion and beauty magazine once said, "There's no such thing as a *slack* French face. I think it's because the French have to exercise their jaws and their mouths so much just to get the words out."

Well, I have no means of testing that statement, but I do know that in an effort to speak French, the whole of the face has to move, whereas the spoken word in English does indeed leave you slack. You can put this to the test — just look in the mirror, and say, "Chérie"! It required effort — exercise. Now say, "Dear". There's no effort needed there.

It reminds me of the words and phrases in common use today — the effortless "Thanks" and even more effortless "Ta" and "Hi!" and "'Bye". The Americans often say, "You're welcome" and, "Have a nice day". Maybe these also tend to be repetitive, but at least more effort is required to say them, and the words themselves have a warmth which makes you smile at the speaker instead of departing poker-faced!

Yes, I must admit I rather like the word "Ché-rie"! Thinking about it can teach us a lot.

THE FRIENDSHIP BOOK

I READ that villagers of Barton-under-Needwood in Staffordshire were asked to "buy a brick" to build a badly-needed parish room. Father David Hutt said, "Like the individual in the community, every brick is important in the building of the church. The good idea behind the brick scheme is that each person who buys one will always have a piece of themselves in that parish room."

If we were honest, most of us would like to feel we have left behind something worthwhile, dreaming perhaps of a best-selling novel, a fine piece of music or an important scientific discovery. These things are achieved by very few, but the many deeds quietly done — helping handicapped people, sparing a few hours of our time to work in a charity shop, being helpful and reliable in our dealings with others — these are all things in which we can make a contribution. They result in those permanent "bricks" which we can be proud to leave behind.

B LESS the Lord, O my soul: and all that is within me, bless his holy name.

Psalms 103:1

A MICROBE is a microscopic organism carrying disease and is found wherever organic matter is in the process of decomposition. I can tell you somewhere else it is found — in gossip! For gossip is the most deadly microbe of all. It has neither wings nor legs, is composed entirely of tales, and most of them have stings.

WHY ARE WE WAITING?

THE FRIENDSHIP BOOK

TUESDAY—OCTOBER 11.

THE editor of "The Barnsley Chronicle" once wrote an article on the Ten Commandments in which he pointed out how invaluable each of them is to human relationships.

He went on to suggest Ten Commandments of his own:

1. Speak to people. There is nothing as nice as a cheerful greeting.
2. Call people by name — not names. The sweetest music is to hear one's name called.
3. Have humility. There is something to be learned from every living thing.
4. Be friendly. If you have a friend — be one.
5. Be cordial. Speak and act as if everything you do is a pleasure.
6. Be interested in others. You can like almost everybody if you try.
7. Be generous with praise, and cautious with criticism.
8. Give your word, then keep it.
9. Be considerate of the feelings of others.
10. Be alert to give service. What counts most in life is what we do for others.

WEDNESDAY—OCTOBER 12.

THERE'S one little word — a tiny word — in the English language which, to my mind, causes more dissatisfaction and grumbles than any other — that tiny word "if".

"I'd be happy *if* I were rich", "*If* I had talent I could do that", "*If* things had been different, I could have . . ." And so it goes on.

Now wouldn't it be splendid *if* we could cut that mischievous word from our thinking? Who knows what we might achieve with a more positive attitude?

THE FRIENDSHIP BOOK

IT was good to see one of our elderly neighbours setting out down the road with her newest little spaniel on the lead. This neighbour has had a long period of ill health and for a time lost all confidence in her ability to go outside on her own, so we were all pleased to see her overcoming the problem and taking Polly out for a walk each day.

A dog has often been called man's best friend, and I read that every fourth household in Britain has at least one dog. Many people have experienced the therapeutic value of owning a dog, and in return for looking after and caring for another living creature, they are rewarded by the constant presence of a faithful companion.

Walt Whitman wrote: "I think I could turn and live with animals, they are so placid and self-contain'd," while Derek Tangye put it this way: "Animals for me represent a form of anchor in my life; a reassurance, a symbol that in this world of envy, greed and humbug, innocence exists".

So here's to the dogs and other creatures in our lives and the pleasure, comfort and loving companionship they give.

FRIDAY—OCTOBER 14.

GIVE me a mind that is not bored,
That does not whimper, whine or sigh.
Don't let me worry over-much
About the fussy thing called I.

Give me a sense of humour, Lord,
Give me the grace to see a joke,
To get some happiness from life,
And pass it on to other folk.
(Anon: found in Chester Cathedral.)

THE FRIENDSHIP BOOK

ISAAC WATTS, the hymn writer, was an academic and a Doctor of Divinity, but in his lifetime he was known as the "Theologian of the Nursery". He advocated simplicity as an approach to teaching religion. Instead of frightening children with threats of punishment if they didn't behave, he showed them how to look on the bright side.

His book, "Divine Songs", became a basis for Sunday School lessons all over the world. It contained rhymes sung to simple tunes — easy for children to remember, and each with a moral — like this one, for instance:

Birds in their little nests agree
And 'tis a shameful sight
When children of one family
Fall out and chide and fight.

AND ye my flock, the flock of my pasture, are men, and I am your God, saith the Lord God.

Ezekiel 34:31

OUR friend Fred is a music lover, and we often hear him playing pieces by the great Polish musician Paderewski.

He reminded me recently of something the composer once said: "If I stop practising one day, I know it. If I stop practising two days, my friends know it. If I stop practising three days, my public knows it."

All budding musicians take note.

THE FRIENDSHIP BOOK

TUESDAY—OCTOBER 18.

A CAMBRIDGESHIRE vicar had been talking about Moses at his family service, and he'd carefully explained how Moses had received the tablets of the Law on Mount Sinai.

At the end of his talk he asked the children, "What did God give Moses?"

"Pills!" shouted one litttle boy enthusiastically.

WEDNESDAY—OCTOBER 19.

I LIKE the challenge enshrined in this little verse:

A bell is not a bell till you ring it,
A song is not a song till you sing it.
Love in your heart is not put there to stay,
Love is not love till you give it away.

THURSDAY—OCTOBER 20.

"I MIGHT be getting on in years and often have to sit in my armchair for hours on end, but that doesn't mean I'm useless," said our old friend, Kate, one day when we went to visit her.

Even as she spoke, her knitting needles were clicking away nineteen to the dozen. She has always enjoyed knitting, but now that her family no longer needs her skills so much, she's found another use for her hobby.

Kate is one of a vast army of knitters all over the country who quietly knit useful squares and hand them in to Oxfam shops to be sewn together as blankets for refugees, the elderly, babies — in fact, any needy person requiring warm covering. They are a group of helpers who don't expect thanks, recognition or rewards — like Kate, they simply get on with the job.

FRIDAY—OCTOBER 21.

THIS verse has been passed on to me by a friend who says that it has been a comfort and encouragement to her in the many perplexities of life — I hope it will be to you, too.

My life is but a weaving, between my God and me,
I do not see the colours He worketh steadily.
Oftimes He weaveth sorrow, and I in foolish pride,
Forget He sees the upper and I the underside.
Not till the loom is silent, and the shuttles cease to
fly,
Will God unroll the canvas and explain the reason
why,
The dark threads are as needful in the skilful
Weaver's hand,
As the threads of gold and silver in the pattern He
has planned.

SATURDAY—OCTOBER 22.

OUR church magazine recently told the story of two small boys who managed to miss the bus home from school. They were six miles away.

The younger boy began to cry, but the elder, who was only eight himself, took hold of his hand and said, "Come on, Davie, it's only three miles each."

Off they marched together. Now, isn't it true that distance doesn't seem as far if you have company along the way?

SUNDAY—OCTOBER 23.

AND then shall they see the Son of man coming in the clouds with great power and glory.

Mark 13:26

THE FRIENDSHIP BOOK

I HAVE just come across a little story about St Francis which I'd like to share with you. It tells that when he sent out his friars to the villages and cities of the world he told them, "Preach the gospel everywhere. Use words if necessary."

This is as true today as it was then — actions so often speak far louder than words, both the written and spoken kind.

TOMORROW

IT'S no good looking backwards —
The cloud which, yesterday,
Darkened the horizon
May not be there today.

It's no good looking backwards,
Reliving loss, or pain —
Tomorrow is a golden day,
To make you smile again.

Anne Kreer.

WHAT a marvellous gift it is to be able to make people laugh, especially in times of tension, or even danger. David Niven, the film actor, had this gift, and he never missed an opportunity to use it.

He was a Major in the Second World War, and took part in the Normandy invasion. As he rallied his troops into action he announced, "Come on, chaps, it's all right for you — but I shall have to go through all this again later, with Errol Flynn!"

THE FRIENDSHIP BOOK

MILLER REESE HUTCHISON, who was born in Alabama in 1876, invented the klaxon horn. He was also the first inventor to market an electric hearing aid. A friend of his, Mark Twain the writer, would tease him by saying that he invented the deafening klaxon to create customers for his hearing aid!

Hutchison's hearing aid was portable and small enough to clip to a belt. Queen Alexandra used one at the coronation of Edward VII to improve her hearing. She was so thrilled with the result, that afterwards she awarded Hutchison a gold medal "for exceptional merit in the field of invention".

Thomas Edison, another great inventor, then made Hutchison his personal assistant at his famous laboratories and he eventually became chief engineer. However, having his hearing aid accepted was always the most rewarding experience in this clever man's life. His pioneering step into a silent world is still helping thousands of people today. Hutchison is a man to be remembered — a true friend of the deaf.

I COULD see by the twinkle in his eye that my young neighbour had another of his riddles for me.

"Mr Gay, why did the orange stop half way down the hill?"

This time I was ready for him. "It had run out of juice!" I replied laughing, for it's not often I get the better of him.

He wasn't finished, though, for he asked another one; "Ah, but how did the orange know the time it ran out of juice?"

I had to admit I didn't know the answer.

"It listened to the pips!"

THE FRIENDSHIP BOOK

YOU sit down to write a letter, then can't think of a thing to say. We've all been in this dilemma. Here's how Iris Hesselden once solved the problem. I commend it to you!

> *What shall I write about,*
> *What shall I say?*
> *My butterfly thoughts*
> *Keep on flitting away.*
> *My notepaper waiting,*
> *My stamps in a line,*
> *The easiest part*
> *Is the name that I sign.*
> *What shall I write about,*
> *What shall I do?*
> *I'll just send a card*
> *Saying, "Thinking of you!"*

AND Jesus said unto him, Receive thy sight: thy faith hath saved thee.

Luke 18:42

IT is a long time since George Stephenson built his successful steam locomotive, but only recently did I come across his personal motto:

"Make the best of everything, think the best of everybody, and hope the best for yourself."

It's well worth thinking about, isn't it? If we look for the best in people, we help them to discover and develop the best in themselves.

Is this not akin to the art of friendship?

NOVEMBER

NOVEMBER must be one of the least favourite of months. It's the time of year when days are shortening, nights are becoming chilly, we are more than likely to see some fog, and the actual feel of the month is in danger of being lost altogether in the anticipation of and early preparations for Christmas.

Yet I like to think of it as the month of remembering. The first day is All Saints' Day when we remember all those saints of the Christian faith — past and present, known and unknown — who have served God faithfully. Next comes Guy Fawkes' Night with bonfires, rockets, sparklers and Catherine-wheels. Then, in the middle of the month, we honour the memory of all those who gave their lives or suffered injury to preserve our freedom.

Finally, November departs with St Andrew's Day, when Scots — wherever they may be — celebrate their Patron Saint. It's not such a dull month, after all, when we stop to think about it!

AT ANY AGE

WE still hold hands and cuddle,
And steal a kiss or two,
And flash each other special looks
That say I do love you.
I suppose you think we're silly,
We're getting on, it's true,
I'm not telling how old I am,
But my husband's seventy-two!

Phyllis Ellison.

THE FRIENDSHIP BOOK

ONE evening every Winter our church holds a poetry evening to raise funds. The Lady of the House is always in her element — she loves it — and I must say that I look forward to it myself.

We live in a country where for hundreds of years, people with lively and sensitive minds have expressed their feelings in poetry, so we have a vast store of works from which to choose, with words that not only sound pleasant, but give an insight into someone else's heart and mind.

We choose our old favourites, both comic and serious — sometimes reminders of emotions we have not touched on for years. It is all very enjoyable, especially discussing the poetry with others.

We ordinary folk, all so different, find that when we come together in friendship and talk about verse, every barrier falls.

LORD BE NEAR ME

THROUGH the tangled web of life,
Lord, guide me.
Through the problems of the day,
Stay beside me.
From the dangers of the world,
Defend me.
When my loved ones slip away,
Befriend me.
In the quiet of the night,
Lord, hear me.
And accept in prayer my thanks
For being near me.

Iris Hesselden.

THE FRIENDSHIP BOOK

WHAT a marvellous thing the mobile library van is, especially for those who are no longer able to carry heavy books for any distance.

I noticed recently that our young library assistant had placed a new notice above her counter:

"Love of books is your pass to the greatest, the purest and the most perfect pleasure that God has prepared for His creatures. It lasts when all other recreations are gone. It will make your hours pleasant to you as long as you live." (Anthony Trollope.)

How true. You're never alone with a good book beside you!

AND early in the morning he came again into the temple, and all the people came unto him; and he sat down, and taught them.

John 8:2

I DON'T know who wrote these lines which appeared in a church magazine, but I think they are worth reflecting upon.

> When as a child sometimes I'd find
> Alone I could not stand,
> My fears just seemed to melt away
> When I held my father's hand.
>
> I'm older and much wiser now.
> More of life I understand,
> But when I'm afraid, I still draw strength
> From my Father's loving hand.

THE FRIENDSHIP BOOK

TODAY I would like to pass on to you a few more thoughts from my collection of points to ponder:

One of the best ways to achieve success lies in turning difficulties into opportunities.

Whenever I feel resentful of growing old, I try to remember that lots of folk have been denied the privilege.

To be 70 years young is sometimes far more cheerful and helpful than to be 40 years old.

Oliver Wendell Holmes.

From the end springs new beginnings.

Pliny the Elder.

If you could kick the person responsible for most of your troubles, you wouldn't be able to sit down for six months.

IT was a bitterly cold evening and the fireside seemed an attractive option, but I knew that our friend Mary would be looking forward to our visit and we were determined not to disappoint her.

"I've a treat for you tonight, Francis," Mary announced as she poured cups of tea. "Joan next door has started cookery classes, and after school she brought me this plate of shortbread. I saved it so that we could enjoy it together."

It was crisp, golden-brown, and delicious.

"You know," smiled Mary later, "a gift doesn't need to be costly to give pleasure. However small it may be, if it's chosen carefully or made with our own hands and given with love, that's all that matters."

Mary never fails to provide us with food for thought.

THE FRIENDSHIP BOOK

LAST Summer we visited the village where I spent my childhood. When we arrived the Lady of the House reminded me that my hair needed a trim, so off I went to the hairdresser.

Three gentlemen were waiting deep in conversation — they did not even see me enter the shop. I sat nearby and overheard their chatter. They were talking about old school friends and their teacher, little knowing that one old chum called Francis whom they had not seen for years was sitting nearby listening!

"Do you remember Jim? He always loved sports and he became a P.E. teacher. Then there was John who was so good at maths, he became an accountant. What about Francis Gay, who liked to write stories? I wonder where he is now?" On hearing this, I hastily introduced myself!

We enjoyed the unexpected reunion, and that overheard conversation reminded me again that we are not only remembered by our names — but by what we do and who we are.

THIS verse has given me plenty to think about over the years. I'm sure you'll enjoy sharing it today.

> *The folk who look happiest,*
> *And those who seem bright,*
> *With smiles on their faces*
> *And feet that are light,*
> *Are not always those*
> *Who have lived in the sun,*
> *But those who faced darkness,*
> *And fought it, and won.*

M

THE FRIENDSHIP BOOK

EVERY year, as is our custom, the Lady of the House and I sit in front of our television, watching the Festival of Remembrance from the Albert Hall in London.

On this solemn occasion, as representatives of the Armed Forces, Nursing Services and Poppy Appeal collectors march with dignity into the arena, we will remember the men and women whose names didn't appear in any lists of awards, whose photos were not published, but who gave of themselves unstintingly.

Rear Admiral Carey Reeve of the United States Navy wrote in his journal: ". . . And this I find the greatest mystery of all — the instinct in man to sacrifice himself that others might live."

So at this time, along with so many others, we offer our silent tribute to all who:

For our tomorrow, gave their today.

AND the seventh angel sounded; and there were great voices in heaven, saying, The kingdoms of this world are become the kingdoms of our Lord, and of his Christ; and he shall reign for ever and ever.

Revelation 11:15

DO you know one of my favourite old songs, "Count Your Blessings"? It reminds us that no matter what our problems might be, we still have a lot to be thankful for.

I was reminded of this when I came across an old story about a man who had two wooden legs. Among his blessings he numbered the ability to keep up his socks with drawing pins!

THE FRIENDSHIP BOOK

USUALLY we speak of "hearing" a good sermon, but it is just as possible to "see" one. I am thinking of a radio talk by Bishop Roy Williamson who gave illustrations of three people he had encountered.

The first was of a lady aged 100 who regularly played the organ in her church and had been doing so for longer than anyone could remember.

Then he recalled the lady in her seventies, recovering from a stroke, but who insisted on seeing the Bishop to her gate. "I'm in training," she explained, "because my friends and neighbours are sponsoring me to walk 300 yards to the post office to collect my own pension. I'm doing it in aid of the homeless."

Finally, there was the blind lady, using a stick and pushing a wheelchair as far as the out-patients' department of the local hospital. She had declined offers of help because it was a service she herself wanted to perform for her husband.

Truly there are many ways to preach a sermon!

MRS Gilbert Force of Park Ridge, Illinois, sent me this thoughtful verse to share with you.

WHISPERING

Among the things that this day brings
May come to you a call —
One which, unless you're listening,
You may not hear at all!
Lest it be soft and low,
Whate'er you do,
Where'er you go —
Be listening!

Wise advice in a noisy world.

THE FRIENDSHIP BOOK

SINCE Emily had a stroke she has not been able to get about very much. She used to wish she had a more interesting view from her window, which looks out on a tiny, enclosed patch of garden. However, the last time I called on her, her eyes were glowing. "Just look!" she said.

Placed right in front of the window was a bird bath, and perched on the edge I saw a blackbird and a pair of chaffinches. When they flew off, other birds fluttered down and took their place.

"They come and go all day," said Emily. "I never knew the names of the different birds, but I've got myself a book so that I can see what they all are. Now *that's* a greenfinch!"

Emily is never bored now. The view from her window has been transformed — and so has her life.

THE Lord's Prayer is very special. For one thing it is the one prayer which almost everyone knows. Though I have recited it all my life, I realised another special feature only when I read this little verse whose author is unknown:

You cannot say the Lord's Prayer and even once say "I",
You cannot say the Lord's Prayer and even once say "my".
Nor can you say the Lord's Prayer and not pray for another,
For when you ask for Daily Bread you must include your brother,
For others are included, in each and every plea,
From beginning to the end of it, it does not once say "Me".

THE FRIENDSHIP BOOK

A DOCTOR should have patience,
And the Lawyer should be brief.
The Farmers ought to have joint talks,
*   If Butchers have a beef.*

The Eye-specialist needs pupils,
*   And the Turkey-Farmer pluck.*
The Weather Forecaster if fair,
*   Is never thunder-struck.*

The Gardener earns our plaudits,
*   If he calls a spade a spade.*
A Draughtsman, who knows where to draw
*   The line, has made the grade.*

We can welcome the Ship's Captain,
*   Who is never all at sea.*
We can relish the Great Actor
*   In what's to be or not to be.*

The Golfer needs a lot of drive,
*   Where fairway pressure's rife,*
And the Footballer, who's eager,
*   Ought to have a goal in life.*

A Banker must show interest
*   In what's going on around.*
A Pilot must have confidence,
*   Or won't get off the ground.*

Such requirements are quite basic,
*   And it's prudent to recall*
That all examples shown provide
*   A message for us all.*

                                    J. M. Robertson.

AND Jesus came and spake unto them, saying, All power is given unto me in heaven and in earth.

                                    Matthew 28:18

THE FRIENDSHIP BOOK

I OWE thanks to Barbara Jemison for these encouraging verses:

You've struck a really cruel bit
Of life's uneven road?
A host of worries burden you?
Yours is a heavy load?

Do not despair — keep on and on,
Another heartbreak mile,
The going may be easier soon —
And one day you will smile.

GEORGE FREDERICK HANDEL was born in Germany and was appointed principal court composer to the Elector of Hanover in 1710. A year or two later, however, he visited England and never returned to Hanover which displeased the Elector greatly.

When the Elector of Hanover became our George I, Handel decided to make amends and wrote a special work in the king's honour. It was "The Water Music" and was performed one July evening by 50 musicians as they sailed down the Thames on the king's barge.

The king was so delighted with the performance that he ordered it to be played three times that evening — twice before and once after supper — even though each performance lasted an hour! The relationship between the king and his court composer was restored.

Today, St Cecilia's Day, let us remember with gratitude the gift of music and its great powers — to soothe, bring solace, to lift our spirits, and to say those things which sometimes mere words cannot express.

THE FRIENDSHIP BOOK

DR WILLIAM BARCLAY, the theologian, teacher and writer, was exceedingly deaf, but he always said that it was a bonus to him. In his study at the bustling and often noisy university where he worked, he would just turn off his hearing aid and then become fully immersed in what he was doing.

We are told, too, of how Beethoven composed in Vienna as Napoleon was bombarding the city. Amid all the terrible noise this deaf man was only aware of the great music pouring from his heart.

If we become engrossed in some interesting activity or if we concentrate on things of beauty and goodness, it is possible for us all to ignore the disturbing and worrying things around us.

This is not just escapism — it is a personal inner victory over outward circumstances.

OUR friend Ben celebrated his 84th birthday recently and at his special party held by friends and relatives, he was asked for his view on life. With his usual good-natured laugh, he announced:

"When I was 14, I was sure I was going to be famous, when I was 24, I was pretty certain I was going be famous, when I was 44, I was 50 per cent sure I was going to be famous. At 64, I was angry because I hadn't become famous, and now at 84 I know it doesn't matter if you're famous or not, as long as you have health, happiness, family and friends."

Ben is right, of course. Fame is no use if you haven't been blessed with these gifts. Possibly the best time in life is when we sit back and count our blessings. Try it today — you'll be surprised how contented you'll feel afterwards.

ELSIE had spent all of her working life as a cleaner at a nearby hospital. She and her husband Ernest had had a happy marriage, although it was a disappointment that they never had children. They were looking forward to Ernest's retirement in a year or two and Elsie was going to give up working also, when illness struck and Ernest became increasingly disabled. It seemed as if all their plans for a happy and fulfilling retirement had fallen to pieces.

Elsie had always been of a timid disposition, depending on Ernest to make the decisions and carry them out, but she loved him dearly and realised that if he was going to enjoy any kind of life outside the four walls of their home, it would depend entirely on her.

So, gritting her teeth, she dipped into her savings and embarked on a course of driving lessons. At first she hated it, but for her husband's sake she was determined to persevere, and at the fourth attempt she was successful in passing her test.

Now, Elsie says, the outings she and Ernest are able to enjoy together make all the effort worthwhile. Truly, a grain of faith and a bit of grit can move mountains!

SATURDAY—NOVEMBER 26.

MOST of us miss out on life's great awards and prizes — the Oscars, the Nobels, the knighthoods. However, don't forget that we're all eligible for life's small awards — the spontaneous kiss, the pat on the back, the sincere thank-you, a place by a warm fire, an enjoyable meal, a glorious sunset.

Leave the grand awards to others, and instead enjoy life's tiny delights. Fortunately, there are plenty for all to receive and, perhaps even more importantly, to give.

FROSTY FINGERS

THE FRIENDSHIP BOOK

JESUS saith unto her, Said I not unto thee, that, if thou wouldest believe, thou shouldest see the glory of God?

John 11:40

MONDAY—NOVEMBER 28.

CHARLES DICKENS rose from a humble background to become the most famous and successful writer of his time. In a comparatively short career he achieved an astonishing output of novels, stories, plays and essays, and yet, in the midst of the punishing work programme he set himself, he was always ready to give time to help others.

A carpenter, John Overs, sent him some songs he had written. Finding out that Overs was self-educated and had a wife and children to support, Dickens advised him against giving up his job for a literary career. However, he also suggested that Overs send the songs to "Tait's Magazine" in Edinburgh. Overs did so and they were published.

From then on, over the years, Dickens often took time in his own busy schedule to assist Overs with revisions of his work. When Overs developed lung trouble, Dickens sent him to his own doctor and helped to pay for the treatment. Afterwards, he found him a light job in a theatre.

Later, when Overs was dying, Dickens arranged with a publisher to bring out a book of Overs' collected poems and songs, and wrote an introduction to it which boosted the sales. After John Overs' death, Dickens rallied his friends to make sure that the widow was not left destitute and that the children were provided for.

Yes, Charles Dickens was a great writer, and he also had a great heart.

THE FRIENDSHIP BOOK

WHEN our friend Winifred came indoors again, after looking round the garden in a blink of winter sunshine, she was singing.

"You sound happy, Winifred," I remarked.

"I'm a happy person. I have everything I need. That doesn't mean I have everything I want — but then that's a different thing entirely."

What a sensible way of looking at things. As Gandhi said, "Earth has enough for every man's need, but not every man's greed."

HOME COMFORTS

A LITTLE taste of luxury,
   A little bit of heaven;
Just you and me, a book, TV,
   The clock at half past seven.

A bowl of fruit, a dish of sweets,
   And music fills the room;
We've closed the curtains, locked the door —
   On outside doom and gloom.

We've written all our letters,
   And friends have been and gone,
We finished all our phone calls
   Before the first star shone.

Let others travel, dance and dine.
   Or seek a warmer shore,
We have our taste of luxury,
   And ask for nothing more!

Iris Hesselden.

DECEMBER

THURSDAY—DECEMBER 1.

A SLOGAN circulating in shops and offices near me announced: "In the interests of economy, the light at the end of the tunnel has been switched off." I couldn't help laughing, but how sad if it were really true.

As many who are going through a time of despondency can testify, the thing that keeps them going is the conviction that a better day will dawn, for as Alexander Pope pointed out: "Hope springs eternal in the human breast." The poet Shelley reminds us: "If Winter comes, can Spring be far behind?" and indeed, whenever did the buds fail to open each Spring, a new day follow the night, or the sunshine come after the rain?

We can be sure that "the light at the end of the tunnel" still burns brightly.

FRIDAY—DECEMBER 2.

WORDS of understanding wisdom come at the most unexpected times — it's remembering them afterwards that's the problem! However, I do remember a remark made to my wife recently, on one of the now infrequent occasions we went to the cinema.

It was a particularly heart-touching biographical film, and when the lights came on at the end we were both dabbing our eyes with soggy tissues. "I feel so silly doing this," said the Lady of the House.

An elderly gentleman sitting in front of us turned round and said, "Madam, don't ever be ashamed to weep at somebody else's misfortune."

Those wise words are ones we'll never forget.

THE FRIENDSHIP BOOK

THOSE two excellent organisations, the Boy Scouts and the Girl Guides, have much in common. I am also quite sure that a healthy rivalry exists between them and many tales could be told of one trying to take a rise out of the other. I must say, speaking as a mere male, that I admire girls when they refuse to be considered the weaker sex.

This story was told to me by a friend who had been in Yorkshire: it was the time for Summer camps and a Boy Scout one had been set up in a meadow. At the site entrance was erected a sign with the name of the troop and its motto, "SECOND TO NONE". Just down the lane a Girl Guide camp had been set up. This, too, at the entrance, had a name sign and the motto, which read quite simply, "NONE"!

THE grace of the Lord Jesus Christ, and the love of God, and the communion of the Holy Ghost, be with you all. Amen.

Corinthians II 13:14

I T could soon become a habit,
And be infectious, too.
You would be held responsible,
For all that it would do.
It would pass from one to another,
And travel many a mile,
And you would be the source of it,
That happy friendly smile.

Phyllis Ellison.

THE FRIENDSHIP BOOK

IN a booklet of old proverbs, two particularly gave me food for thought:

The sooner the better — delay is a fetter.

What may be done at any time will be done at no time.

They are a reminder that time flies and if all our good intentions are to succeed, then it is a good idea to make a start on them. Emily Dickinson expressed a similar thought more poetically.

If I can stop one heart from breaking,
I shall not live in vain;
If I can ease one life the aching
Or cool one pain;
Or help one fainting robin
Into his nest again
I shall not live in vain.

More recently David Grayson wrote: "I sometimes think we expect too much of Christmas Day. We try to crowd into it the long arrears of kindliness and humanity of the whole year. As for me, I like to take my Christmas a little at a time, all through the year."

I forget who wrote the following, but it sums it up perfectly: "Today well lived makes every yesterday a dream of happiness and every tomorrow a vision of hope."

WHEN the Lady of the House and I visited a lovely garden on an Open Day recently, we stopped beside a sundial, and were impressed by the inscription around the face. I memorised the words to pass on to you:

The hours fly,
Flowers die,
But love lives on for ever.

THE FRIENDSHIP BOOK

HAVE you heard the story about the small boy who wandered into a church one weekday to have a look round? On his return home his mother asked where he had been.

"Well," he replied, "I just popped into church. I didn't see God there — but His wife was dusting the pews!"

IN our more relaxed society the stolen kiss under the mistletoe is not the popular custom it once was, yet for old times' sake I still like to include a sprig of mistletoe amongst our Christmas decorations.

A Norse legend tells that the beautiful god Baldur was slain by a dart made from the mistletoe bough. In their grief all created things wept and their tears, like drops of pearl, were collected and returned to the tree which had been the cause of Baldur's death — the mistletoe berries which we see today.

Some people believe that the cross on which Christ was crucified was made from the wood of the mistletoe, and afterwards it drooped its fruit in shame and shrank to its present size. Certainly it is not customary to use it in the decoration of churches and it was barred altogether in the times of Calvin and Cromwell because of its pagan origins. In some countries girls would place a sprig of mistletoe under the pillow hoping to dream of the man they would marry!

The dark green leaves and pearly white berries make a handsome decoration for our home and if it is hung with the idea of encouraging our loved ones to exchange goodwill kisses beneath it — then I am all in favour of tradition!

WINTER WOOLLIES

THE FRIENDSHIP BOOK

IT is over 100 years since Jane Laler died. I had never heard of her before, but a friend visiting Kentucky spotted a lonely gravestone with an inscription which would not have won many prizes for spelling:

Jane Laler, ded Agus 1879. She wuz allus kind to everybuddie.

Reading between the lines of that rough inscription, we can sense that Jane Laler was one of God's humble folk who endeared herself to everyone.

It reminded me of the wise counsel offered by a minister: "So live that you will be missed."

Isn't that some encouragement for many of us who are never likely to hit the headlines, but who try to be kind to everybody, and as a result exert an influence far beyond anything they may have realised?

BUT if the Spirit of him that raised up Jesus from the dead dwell in you, he that raised up Christ from the dead shall also quicken your mortal bodies by his Spirit that dwelleth in you.

Romans 8:11

THE simple things
Are often best:
A simple,
Helping hand,
A kindly thought,
The simple phrase,
"Of course I understand."

Anne Kreer.

N

THE FRIENDSHIP BOOK

PEOPLE in Austria, I am told, have a delightful custom that I haven't come across anywhere else.

In the period before Christmas when they are visiting friends and relatives, they take with them a little decoration to hang on the Christmas tree. These are inexpensive and usually very personal home-made things — prettily-decorated fir cones, trinkets, tiny dressed dolls, hand-painted wooden toys or little packages done up in fancy paper and shiny ribbon.

These little gifts are kept carefully and used year after year, each one a reminder to the family of Christmases past and happy memories of the giver.

WHEN I pulled back the curtains one morning, it was a dull, drab, rainy day. It made me feel rather low, for it was the weekend and I had planned to do some gardening.

How should I use the time now? It looked as though the rain was here to stay, so after wandering around rather aimlessly after breakfast, I found a pile of old books lying in a corner. Here was a golden opportunity to sort them out!

As I scanned through some of the pages, I found this verse by James Russell Low:

Every morning lean thine arm awhile
Upon the window sill of heaven,
And gaze upon thy God.
Then with the vision in thy heart,
Turn strong to meet the day.

I hated the thought of clearing out books which had once been familiar old friends, but finding this timely piece of good advice helped me to find exactly the right perspective.

A DREAM IN YOUR HEART

K EEP a dream in your heart
And you'll never be old.
Let the wonder of childhood
Enrich and enfold.
Let the spirit of Christmas
Refresh and renew,
And the promise of New Year
Be hopeful for you.

Remember the rainbow
When storm clouds appear,
And seek the first star
When the ev'ning is near.
Though years are relentless,
Just let them unfold,
Keep a dream in your heart —
And you'll never be old!

Iris Hesselden.

SIX-YEAR-OLD Sam was busy writing Christmas cards for his friends, but suddenly stopped and closed his eyes while he felt one of the cards.

"This won't do for Andrew," he said, thinking of the little blind boy in his class.

"What sort of card would be suitable?" asked his mother.

"A feely one," replied Sam. So they cut out stiff card in the shape of a tree, and added crumpled crepe and tinselled string as decoration.

I'm told that Andrew was thrilled with his "feely" card which got a special place by his bed. He knew he has a real friend in Sam.

THE FRIENDSHIP BOOK

AT Christmas the Lady of the House likes to visit churches nearby to see the floral decorations and the little cribs, all so alike, yet all so different, too, with their specially-crafted Shepherds and Wise Men.

These visits to other churches usually end with us looking through the visitors' books. How revealing they can be. People come from all over the world to see our old churches, and, while you and I are otherwise occupied, they stop to say a little prayer in the peaceful atmosphere.

In these days of upheaval and turmoil it is sometimes difficult to believe that there are still so many people who set aside time to pray, but the church visitors' books show us that indeed there are.

SUNDAY—DECEMBER 18.

AND suddenly there was with the angel a multitude of the heavenly host praising God, and saying, Glory to God in the highest, and on earth peace, good will toward men.

Luke 2:13-14

MONDAY—DECEMBER 19.

AT one of the coldest times of the year, let us not forget all the little creatures that come into our gardens — and their needs — as this old verse by an unknown author reminds us:

God bless the little things at Christmastide,
All the little wild things that live outside;
Little cold robins and rabbits in the snow,
Give them good faring and a warm place to go;
All the little young things for His sake, Who died,
Who was a Little Thing, at Christmastide.

SNOW AND REINS

THE FRIENDSHIP BOOK

THE Kent poet Noel Scott occasionally sends me a few of his verses. This one particularly caught my eye and my fancy:

Don't start to worry:
It's sure to upset you.
Like riding a rocking-horse,
Where does it get you?

A WEEK or two before Christmas each year, I buy a present for the Lady of the House — a poinsettia. With its scarlet bracts and dark green leaves it looks well on our sitting-room table and helps to create the right mood for our Christmas decorating.

Of all the plants available at Christmas, it is probably the most popular. It originates from Mexico and was named after Joel Roberts Poinsett, a former American Ambassador to Mexico.

There is a lovely legend about the poinsettia. On Christmas Eve it was the custom for all the children of the village to take a bunch of flowers to place at the crib of the Christ Child. However, one little girl was so poor that she had no flowers to offer, and so she sat by the roadside weeping. Suddenly, an angel appeared at her side, and finding out the cause of the child's unhappiness, told her to pick a bunch of grasses from the wayside and take them to the church. Drying her eyes the girl did as she was bid, and as she placed her gift in front of the crib, the grass was transformed into the most beautiful bunch of poinsettias.

As I say, it is just a legend, yet it is still true that when faith and love combine at Christmas, very special things can happen.

A very happy Christmas to you!

THE FRIENDSHIP BOOK

*C*HRISTMAS *carols sung by children*
  With enthusiastic voice,
Spreading far the Yuletide message
  Helping every heart rejoice,
As the family parties gather
  Round the hearth to re-unite,
Where the season's reminiscing
  Kindles memories to delight.
Now the church bells ring to welcome
  Folk at home, and those away,
Linking thoughts of celebrations
  On this new, and festive day!

Elizabeth Gozney.

ACCORDING to legend, the robin was once a dull-coloured bird without the red breast that distinguishes it from other birds.

On the night that Jesus was born in the stable at Bethlehem, it was very cold. Mary was worried that her baby son would not be warm enough, so Joseph made a fire and they lay down beside it to sleep.

A little bird was watching them through a crack in the roof and saw that the fire had begun to die. Flying down, he tried to replenish it, but the wood was too heavy for him to lift. So, all night long he stood by the fire, fluttering his wings to keep the flames bright.

When morning came, Mary saw that the robin's breast was reddened by being too close to the blaze.

"You brave little bird!" she exclaimed. "In recognition of your courage and devotion, you shall keep your red breast forever, and then everyone will know how you risked your life for your Lord."

THE FRIENDSHIP BOOK

ONE Christmas Eve a choir from my church was going the rounds singing carols to raise money for a national children's charity. Before the singers reached our road, a group of local children had already visited us, singing carols, but keeping any donations as pocket money.

Later in the evening they heard about the church group. Soon afterwards, they came a second time to our door. As I answered their knock, the eldest child said, "We'd like to give the money we collected for those needy children, too. Will you make sure they get it, please?"

Truly, Christmas had begun in their hearts.

WHEN they had heard the king, they departed; and, lo, the star, which they saw in the east, went before them, till it came and stood over where the young child was.

Matthew 2:9

FRIENDSHIP

SOME paint lovely pictures,
Others write good books,
Some make peaceful gardens,
Others are fine cooks.
But the talent that endureth,
That matters in the end,
Is the tenderness and caring
That makes a faithful friend.

Jean Harris.

WHERE THE HEART IS

THE FRIENDSHIP BOOK

AN INITIAL SURVEY

WHENEVER trouble beckons,
As it sometimes likes to do,
It's handy to remember
Understanding starts with "U".

Though prejudice is lurking
Here and there, it's also true
Its presence can be challenged —
Unbiased starts with "U".

If adversity should threaten,
Here's the safest thing to do —
Tackle it with courage,
Unflinching starts with "U".

Caring comes with sharing,
It's a potent point of view
With its basic explanation—
Unselfish starts with "U".

Support to fight the blues requires
Enthusiasm plus.
Unanimous begins with "U",
And ends, dear friends, with "us".

J. M. Robertson.

I COULD tell that the young lad next door had a riddle for me when he called over the garden fence.
"Mr Gay, why did the little biscuit start to cry?"
"I don't know."
"Because his mother was *a wafer* so long."
Crumbs!

THURSDAY—DECEMBER 29.

*W*HEN the going's very hard
Because the road is rough,
Can you keep on keeping on?
Can you do your stuff?
Yes — surprisingly perhaps,
Travelling can be fun
If you're loved by someone who
Sometimes says, "Well done!"

FRIDAY—DECEMBER 30.

OUR Baptist church had an outing one day — and ended up at a fine old castle. On the top storey, our friend John met an elderly crippled lady.

"Didn't you find it a bit difficult to get up here?" he asked.

"Yes," she said smiling, "but I managed — by taking one step at a time."

There's a lot that can be done, isn't there, if you approach problems this way.

SATURDAY—DECEMBER 31.

THE start of a New Year gives us a clean sheet and an opportunity to make changes.

I would like to pass on, as food for thought, something by the essayist Charles Lamb:

"The man who does not at least propose to himself to be better this year than he was last, must be either very good or very bad indeed."

When David Livingstone offered himself for missionary service, he was asked where he was willing to go.

"I will go anywhere," he said, "so long as it is forward."

A good resolution indeed.

Where The Photographs Were Taken

A LESSON FOR LIFE — *The Falls Of Falloch, Perthshire.*
WINTER EXPEDITION — *Daws Hill, High Wycombe.*
FROST FANTASIA — *The River Wey, Burpham, Sussex.*
WINTER'S MANTLE — *Clifton Hampden, Oxfordshire.*
SPRING IS IN THE AIR — *Girthon Church,*
Gatehouse of Fleet.
FLOWERS AND FEATHERS — *Sheffield Park, Sussex.*
THE FORCE OF NATURE — *Skelwith Falls, Cumbria.*
OUR WORLD — *Lough Tay, Co. Dublin.*
DISTANT HORIZONS — *Brill Windmill,*
Buckinghamshire.
VALE OF PEACE — *Upwey, Dorset.*
PLEASURES — *The Kennet And Avon Canal,*
Little Bedwyn, Wiltshire.
WHEN DAY IS DONE — *Crinan Canal, Argyll.*
PATTERNS IN STONE — *Giant's Causeway, Co. Antrim.*
PRECIOUS MOMENTS — *Loch Garry, Inverness-shire.*
TWO WORLDS — *Lower Slaughter, Gloucestershire.*
PARADISE FOUND — *The Home Of Thomas Hardy,*
Stinsford, Dorset.
BRIGHT HAVEN — *Tobermory, Isle of Mull.*
FAMILIES AFLOAT — *Hambleden Mill, River Thames.*
RAINBOW ROAD — *Near Flisk, Fife.*
FROSTY FINGERS — *River Windrush, Burford,*
Oxfordshire.
WINTER WOOLLIES — *Bagendon, Gloucestershire.*
SNOW AND REINS — *Shamley Green, Surrey.*

ACKNOWLEDGEMENTS: **David Askam;** Winter Expedition, Apple Blossom Time, Bright Haven. **Ivan Belcher;** Winter's Mantle, Distant Horizons, Pleasures, Togetherness, Precious Moments, Two Worlds. **Paul Felix;** Making Friends, Carved With Pride, Paradise Found, When Day Is Done, Families Afloat, Frosty Fingers, Winter Woollies. **V. B. Hicks;** A Lesson For Life. **Picturepoint;** Patterns In Stone. **Clifford Robinson;** Against The Grain. **John Rundle;** Spring Is In The Air, Rainbow Road. **Kenneth Scowen;** Autumn Woods. **Andy Williams;** Frost Fantasia, Flowers And Feathers, The Force Of Nature, Vale Of Peace, Why Are We Waiting?, Snow And Reins, Where The Heart Is.

Printed and Published by D. C. THOMSON & CO., LTD.,
185 Fleet Street, London EC4A 2HS.
© D. C. THOMSON & Co., Ltd., 1993

ISBN 0-85116-570-2